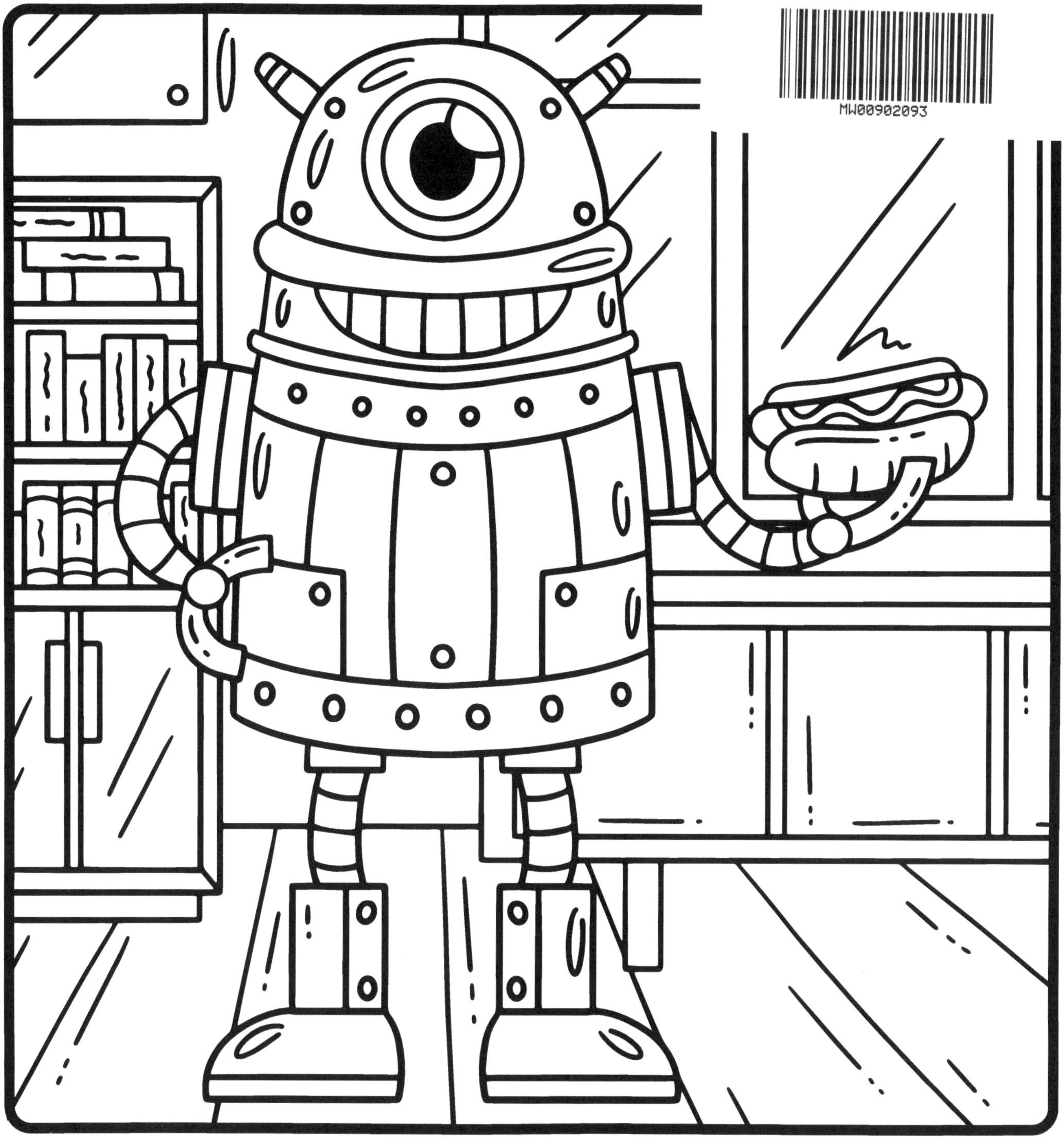

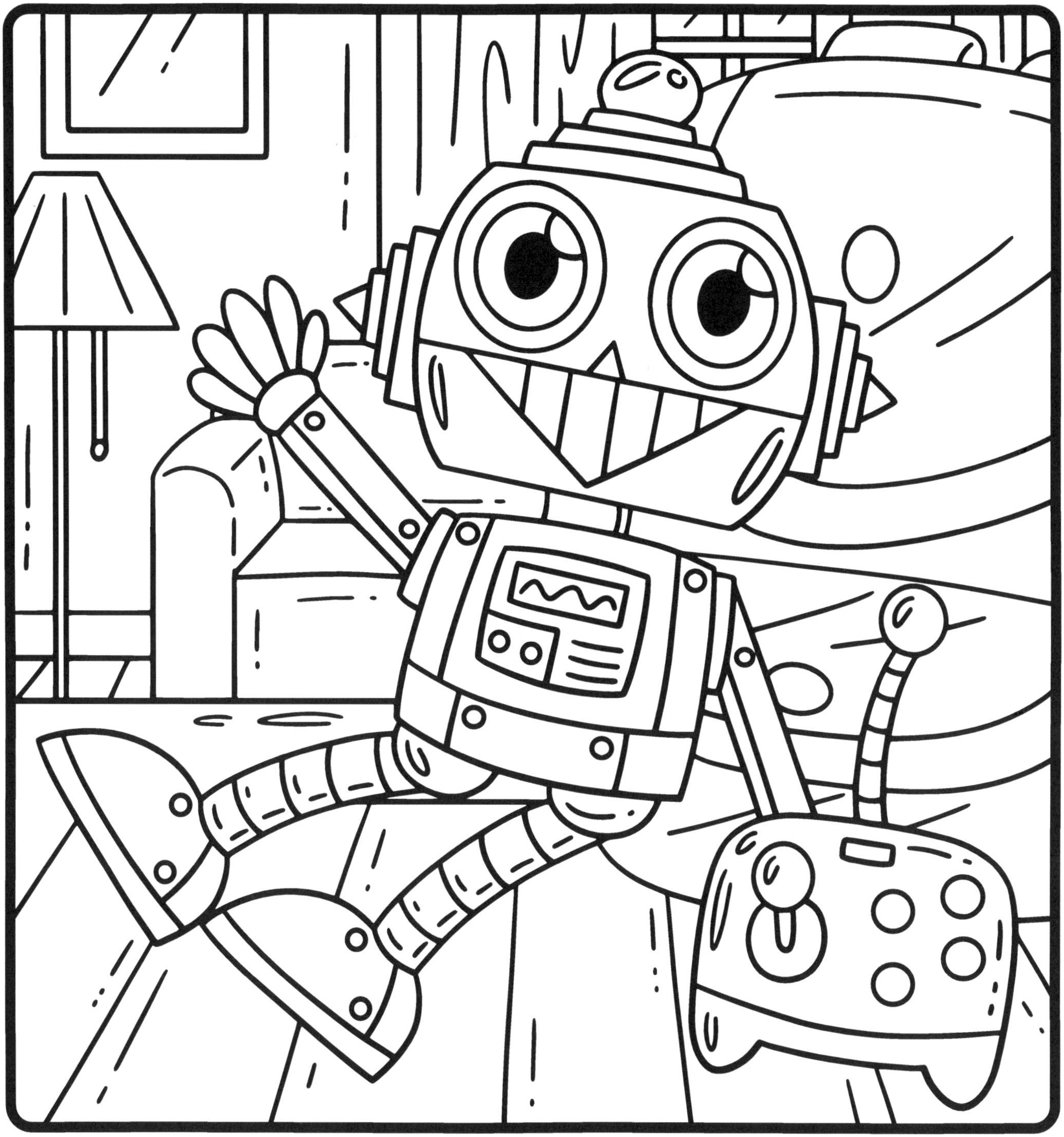

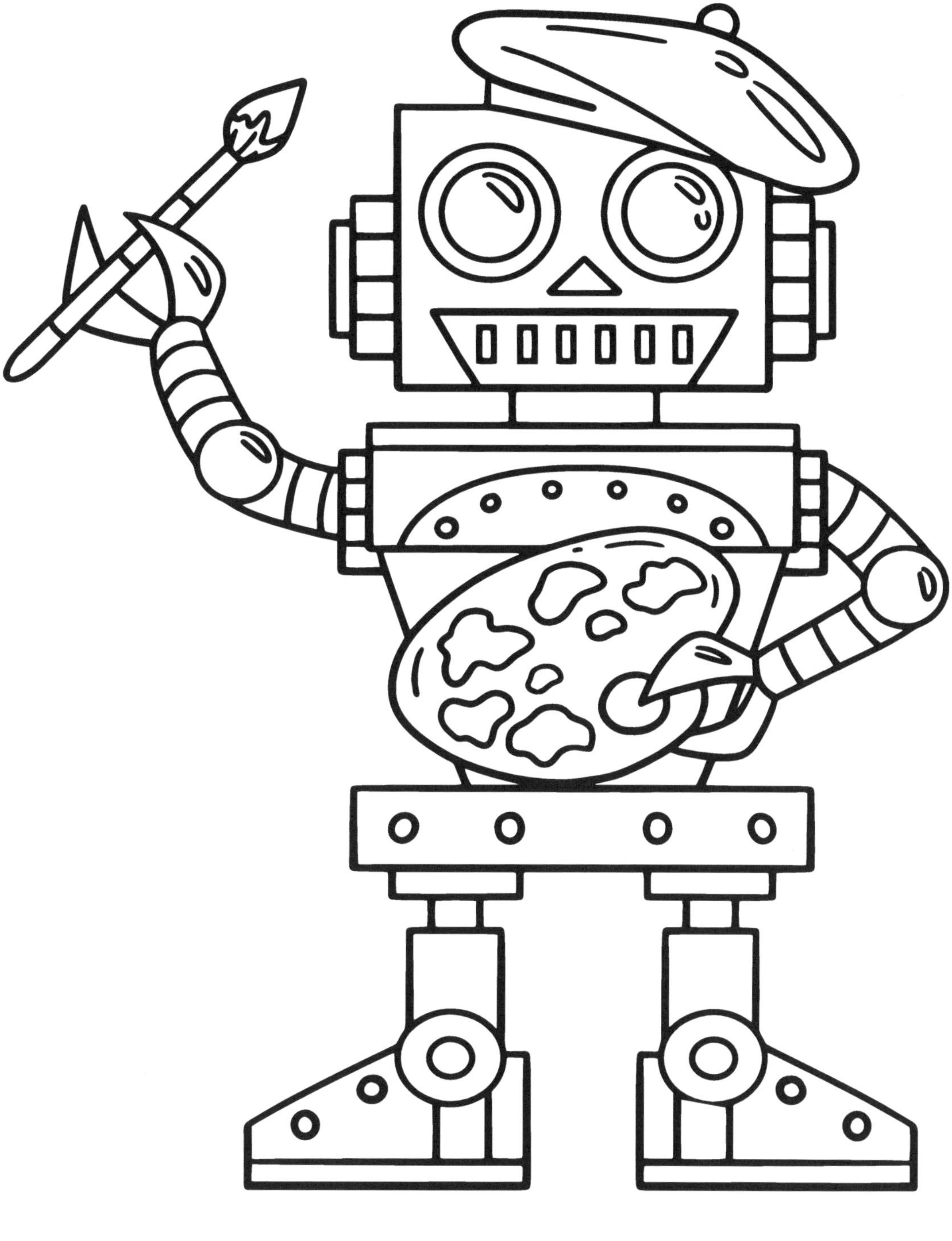

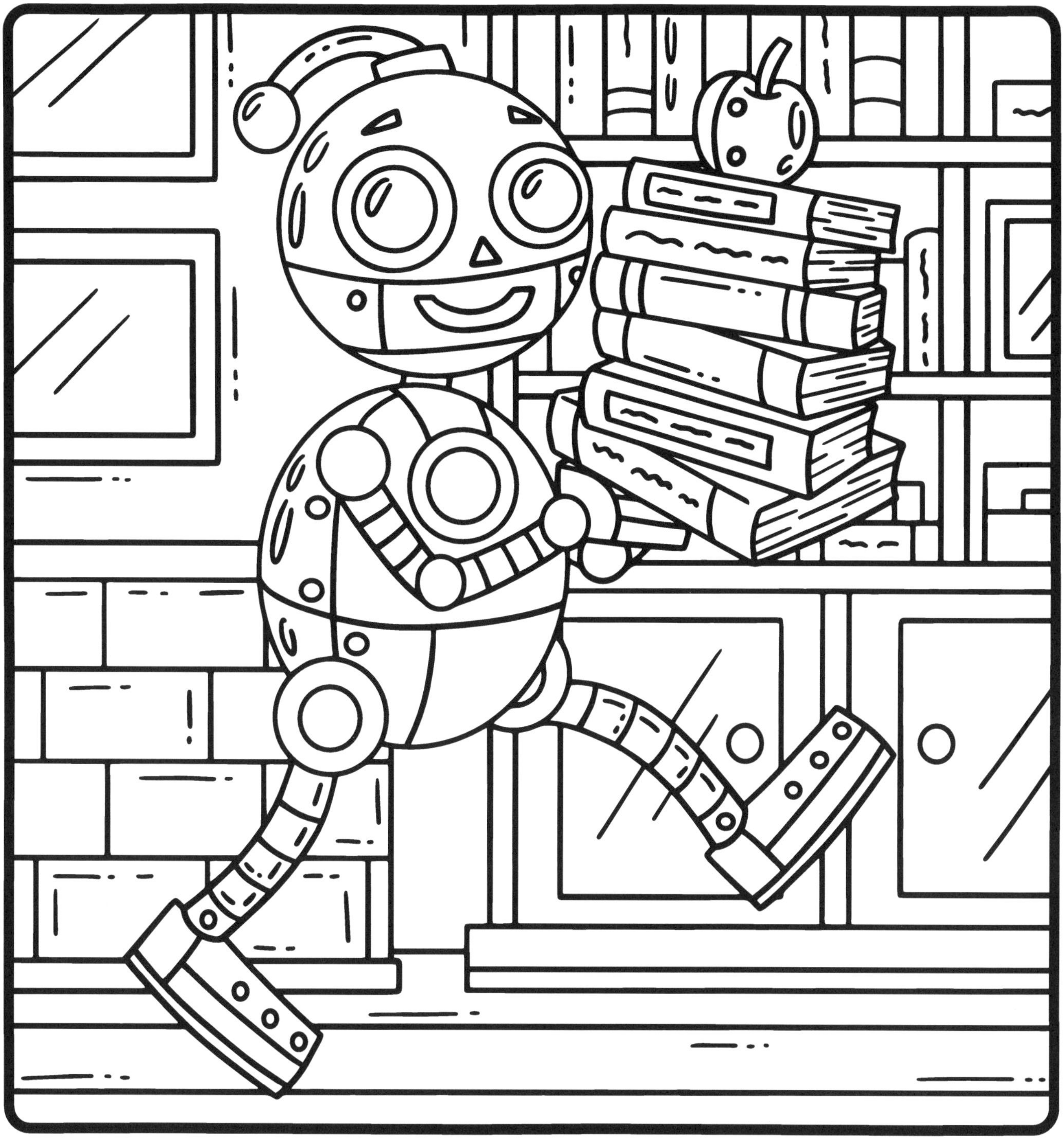

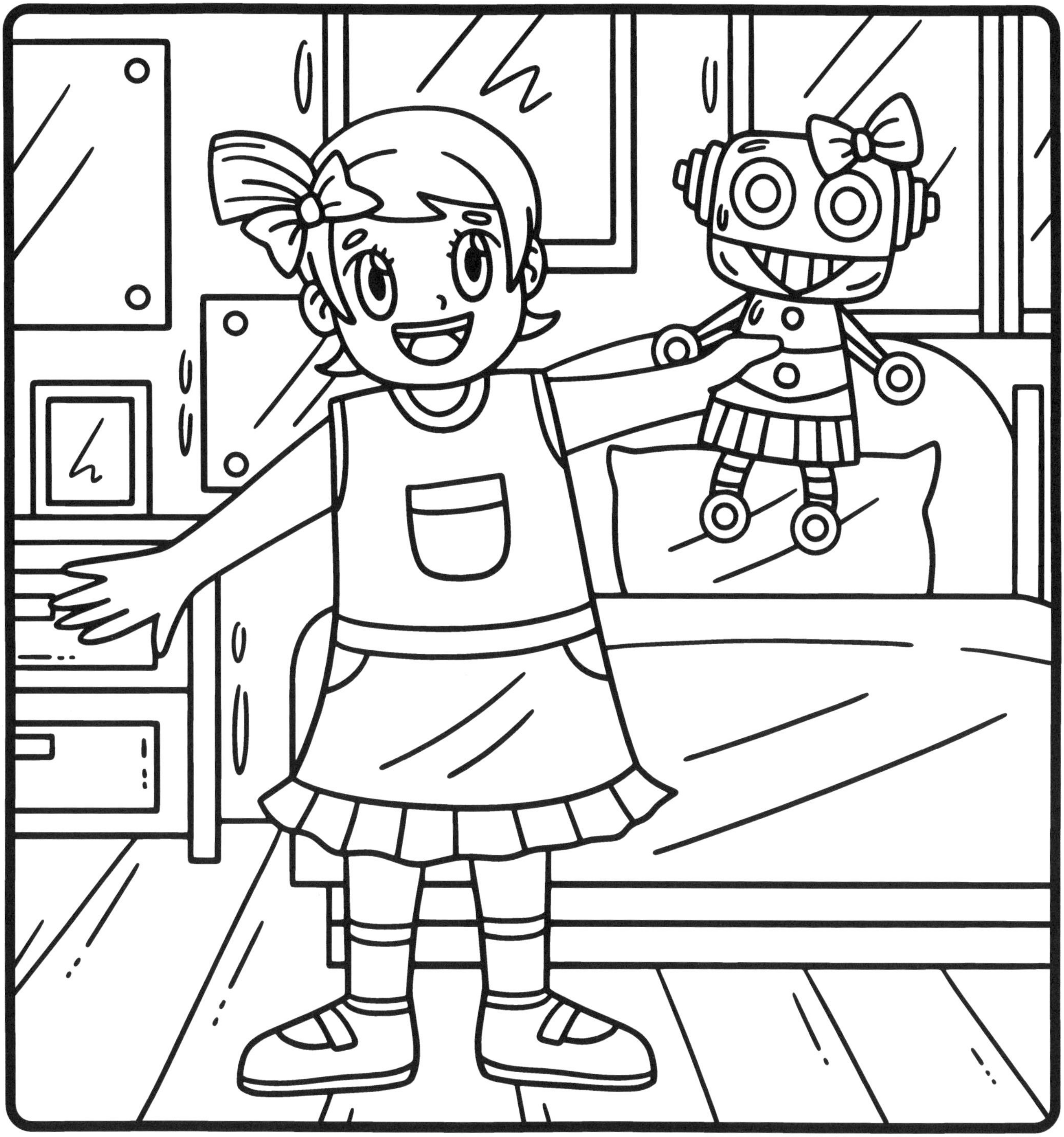

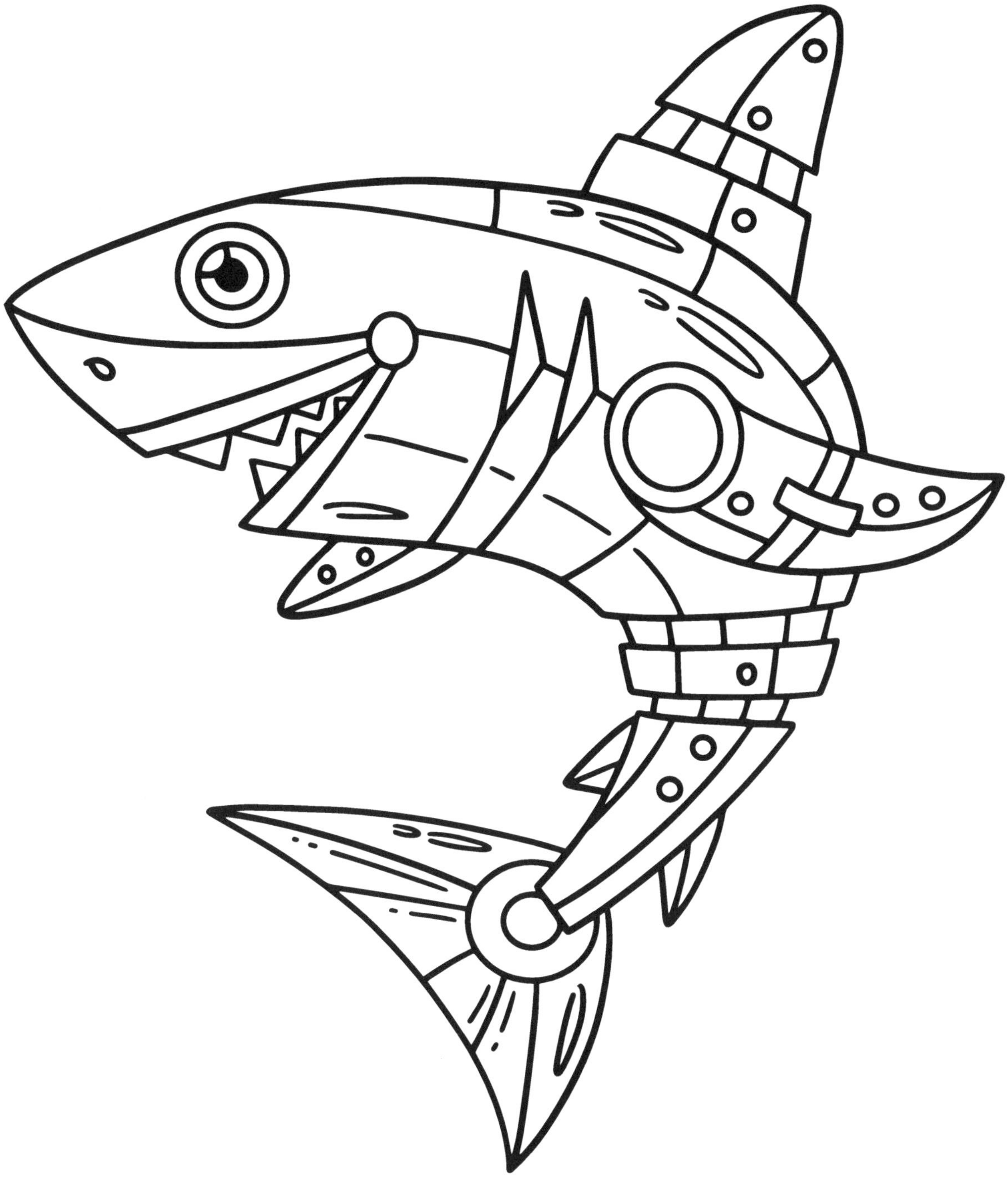

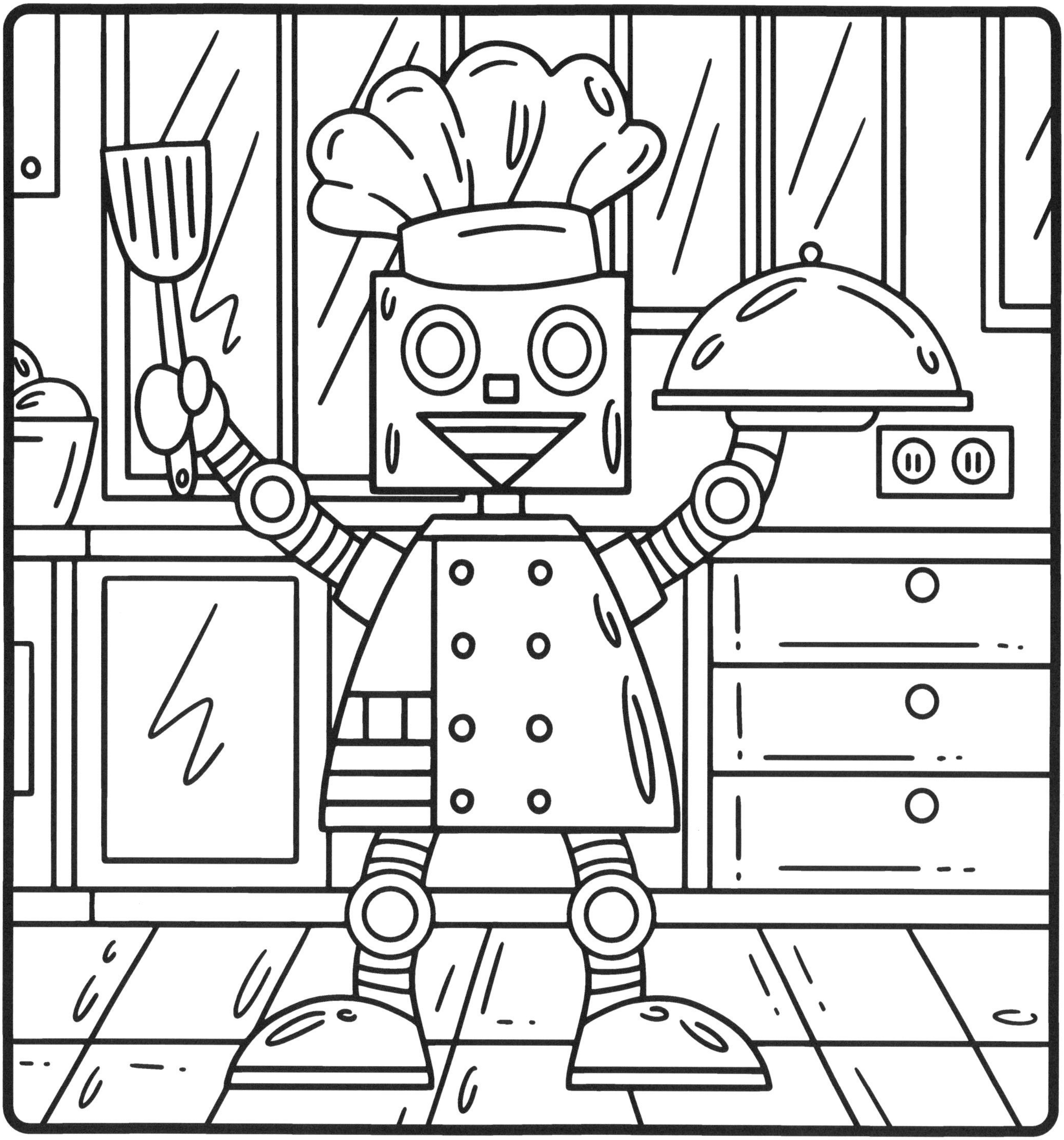

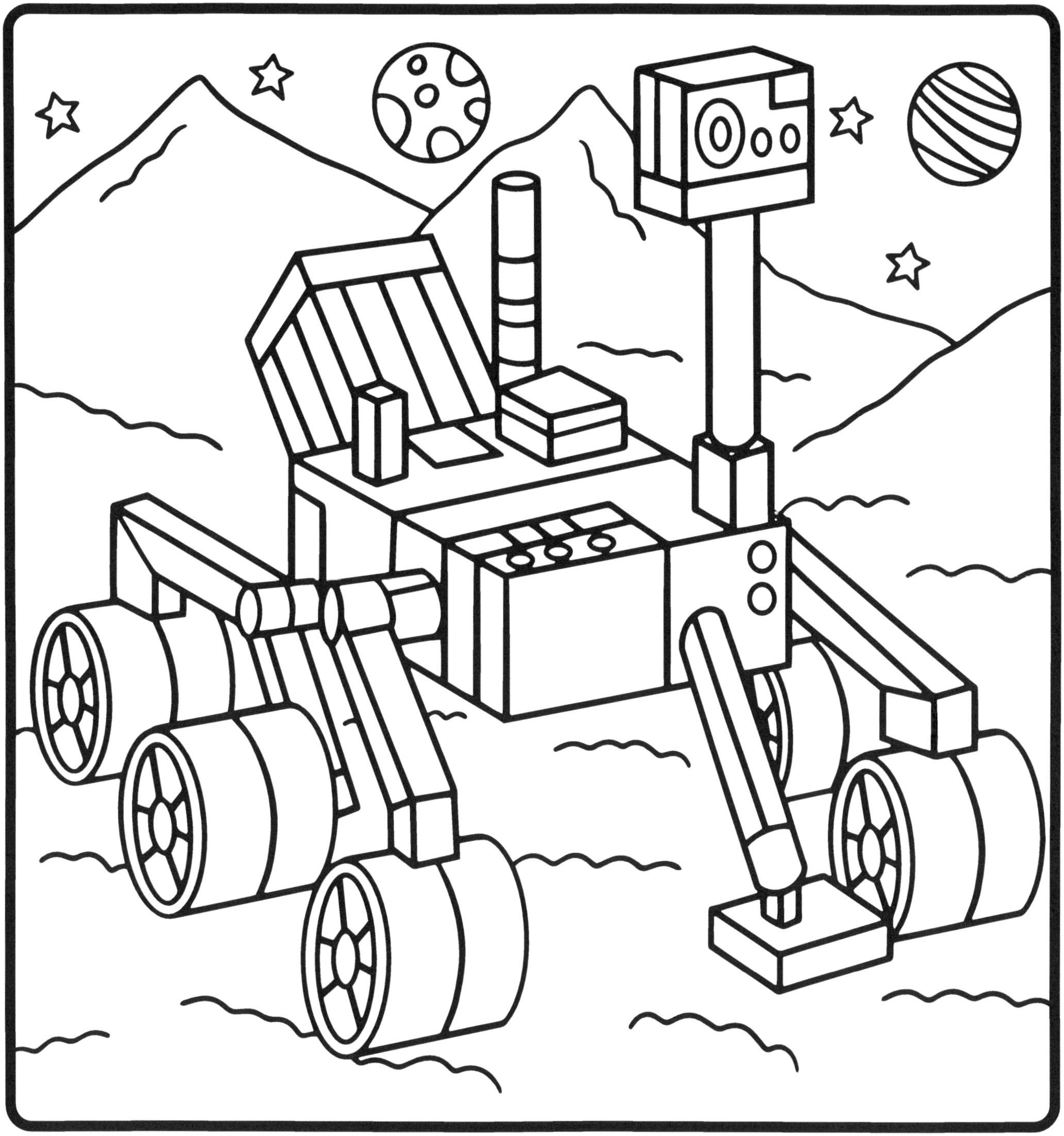

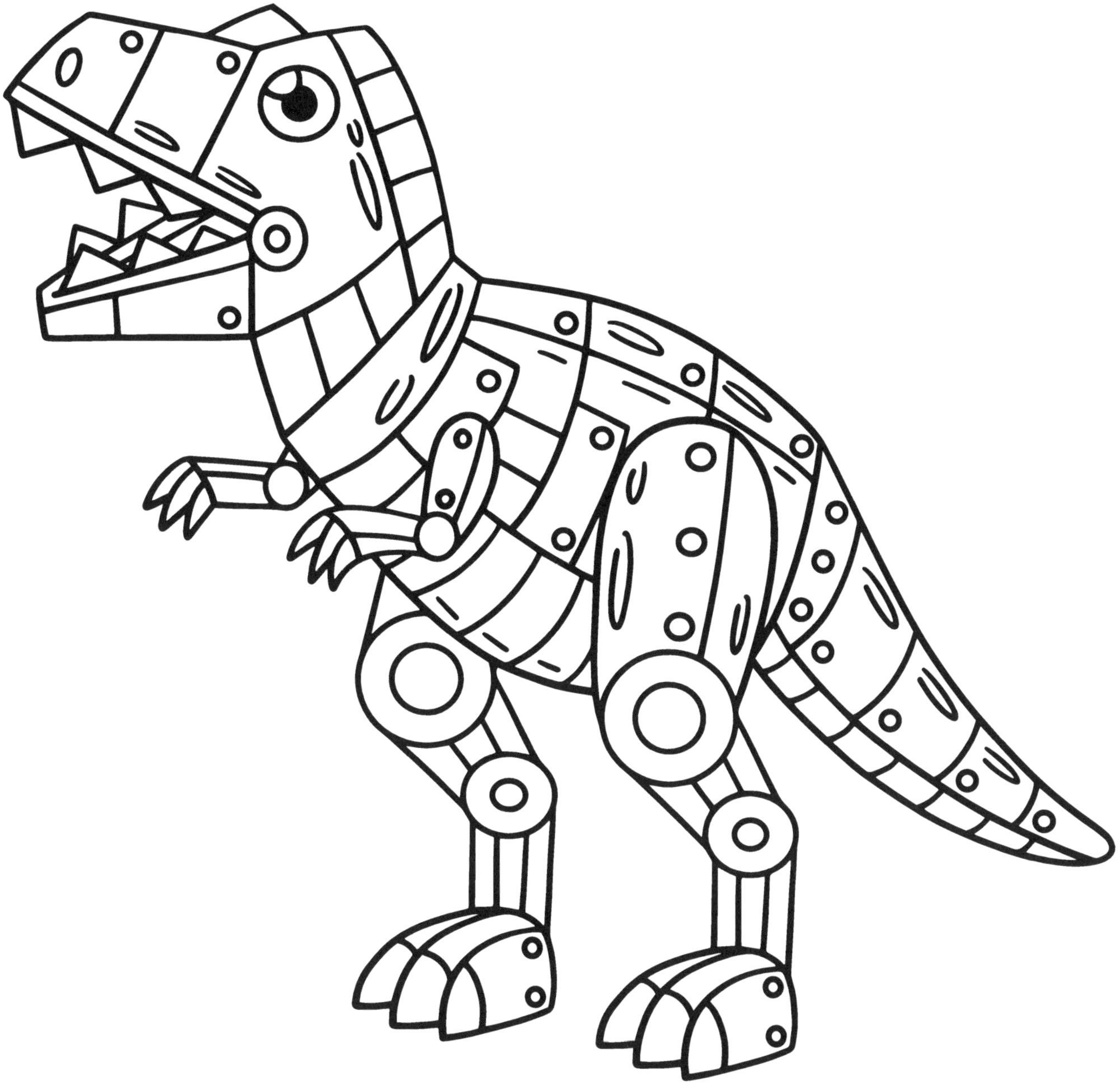

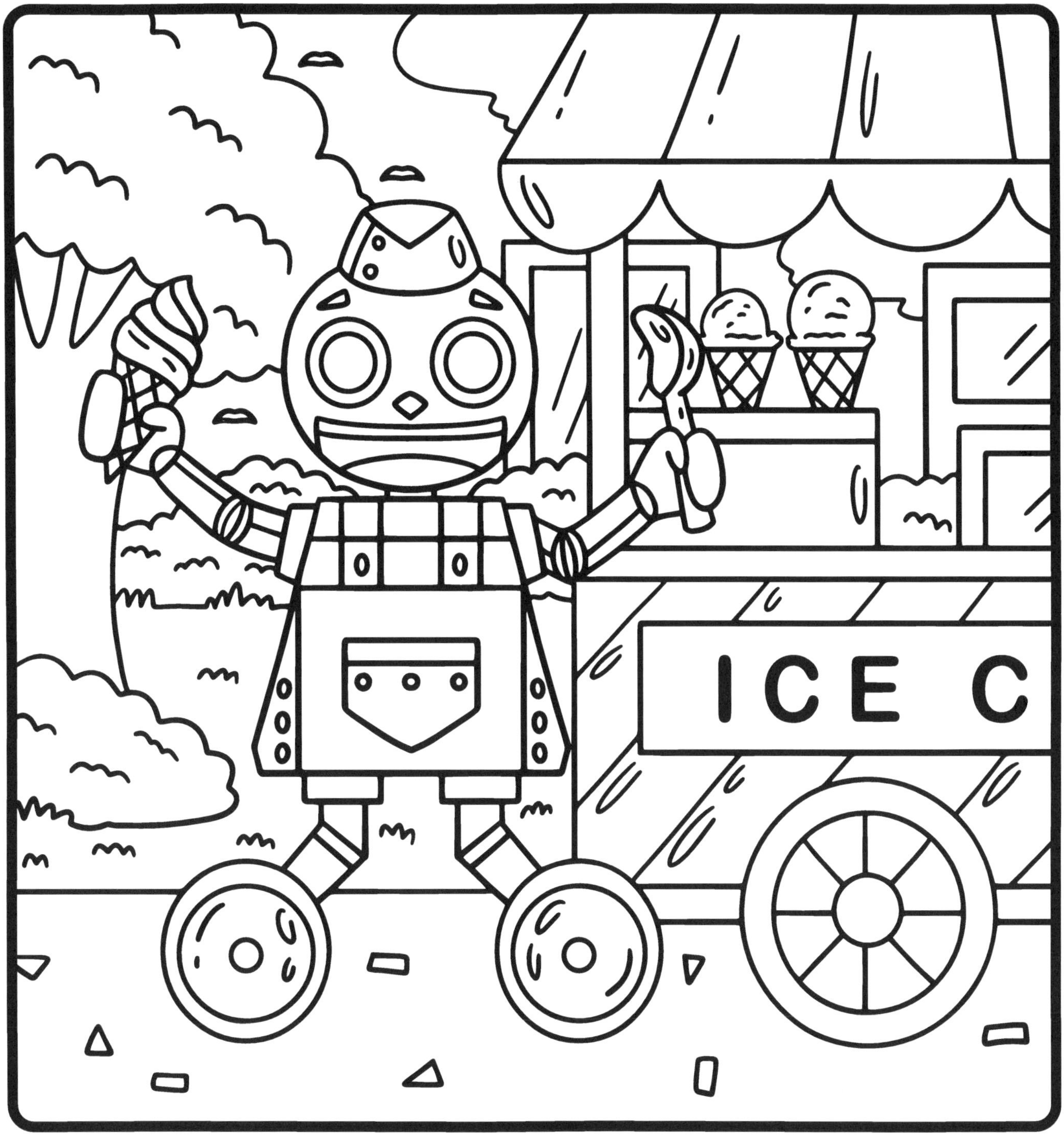
ICE C

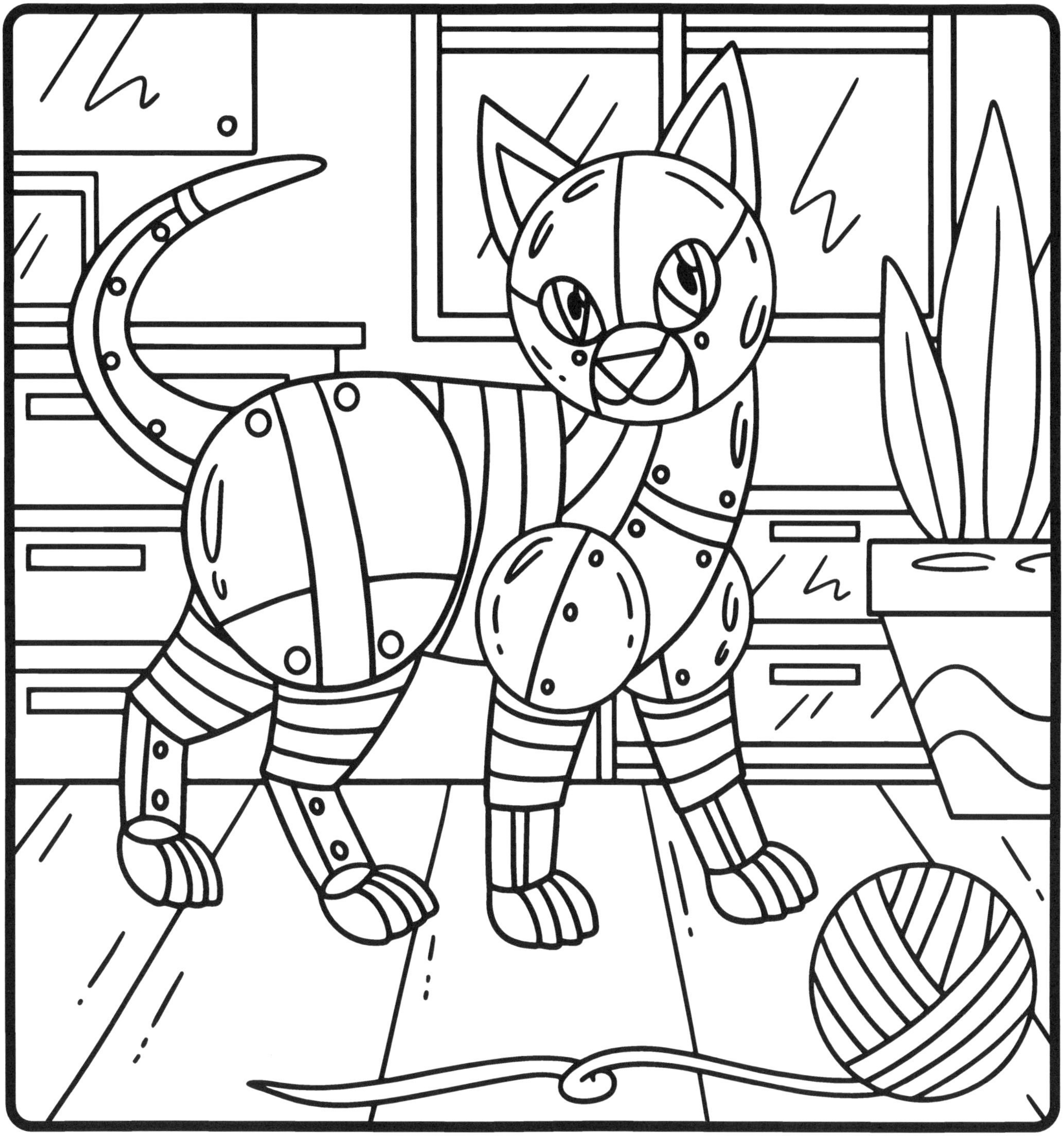

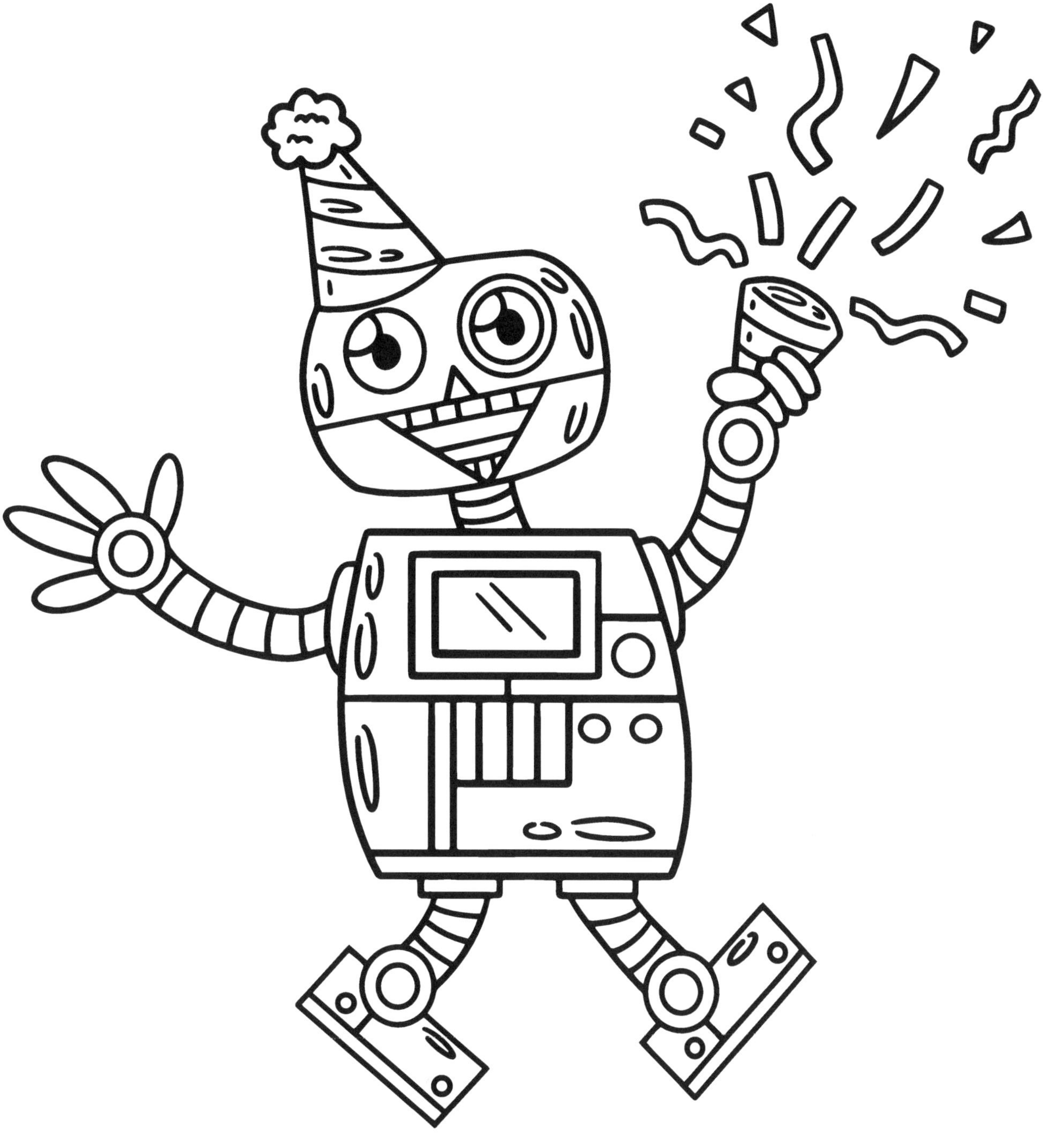

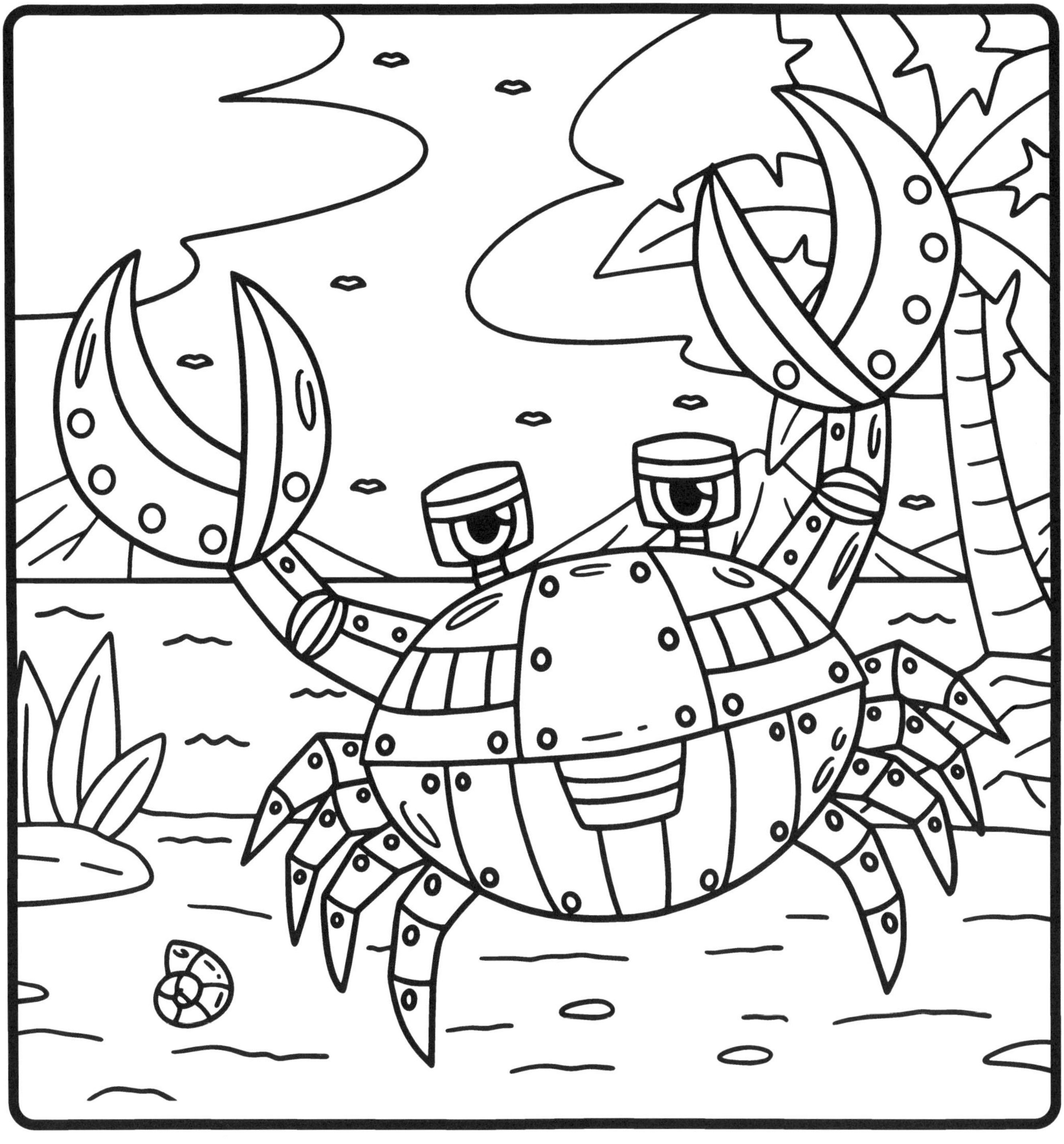

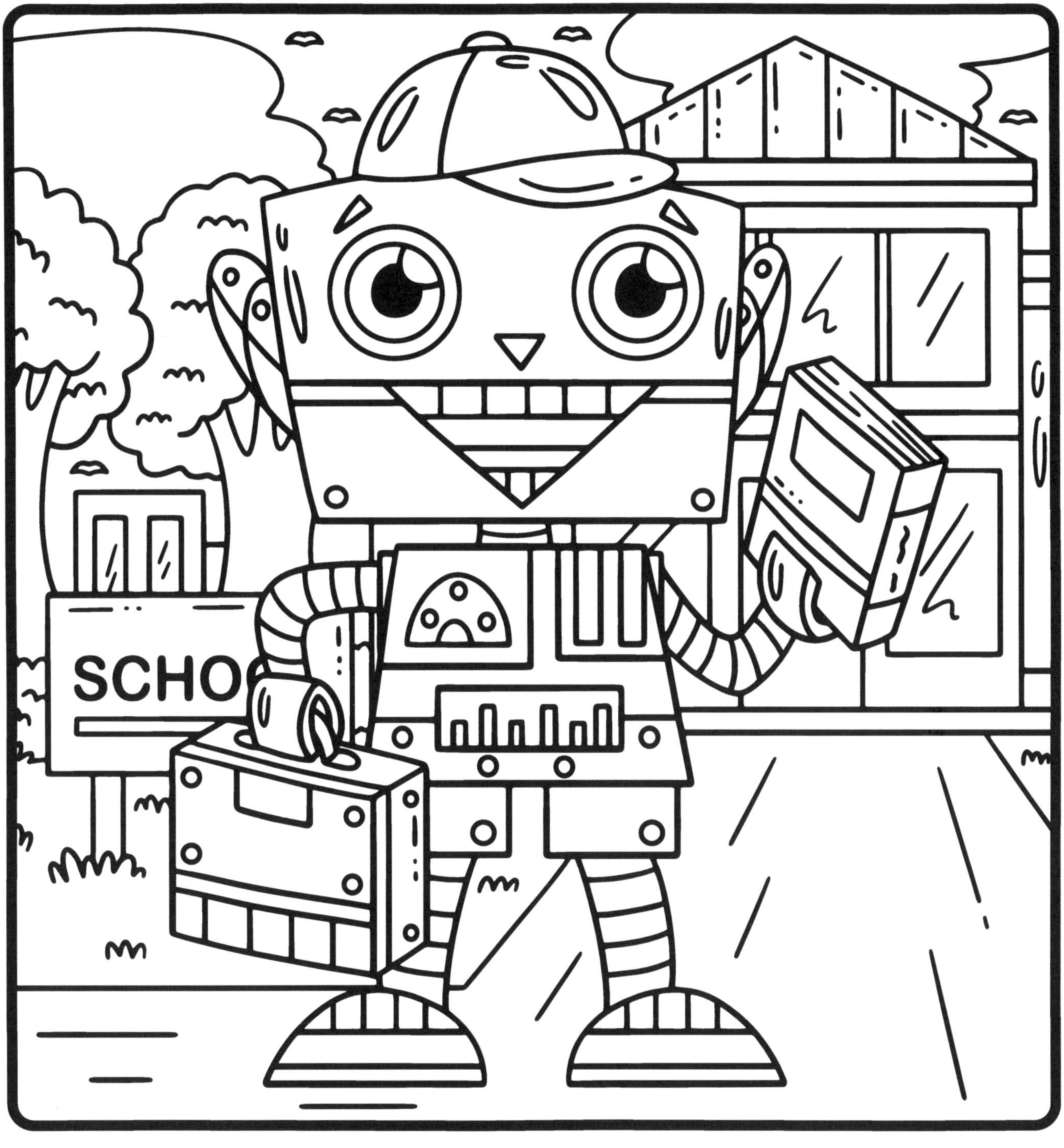
SCHOO

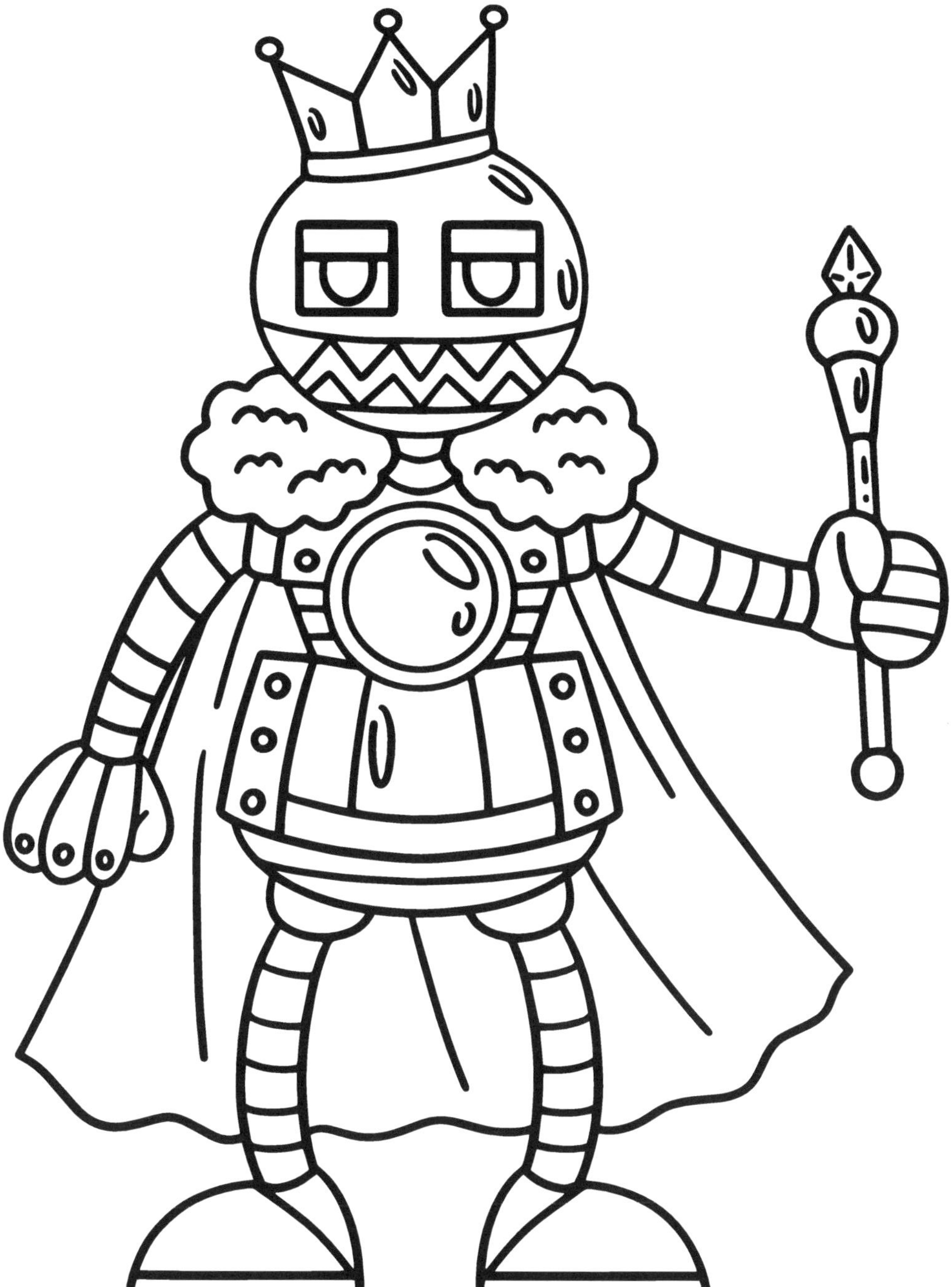

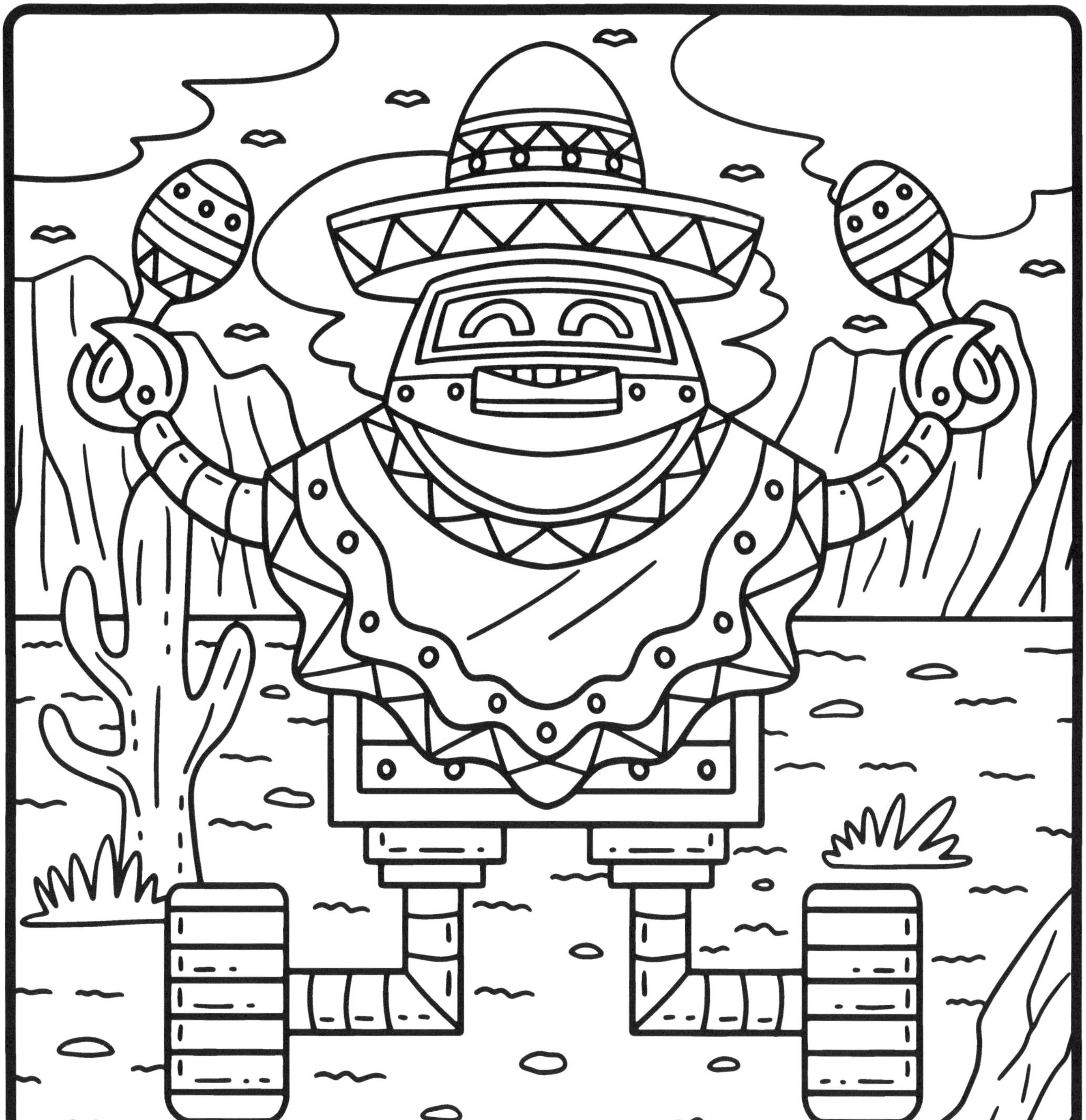

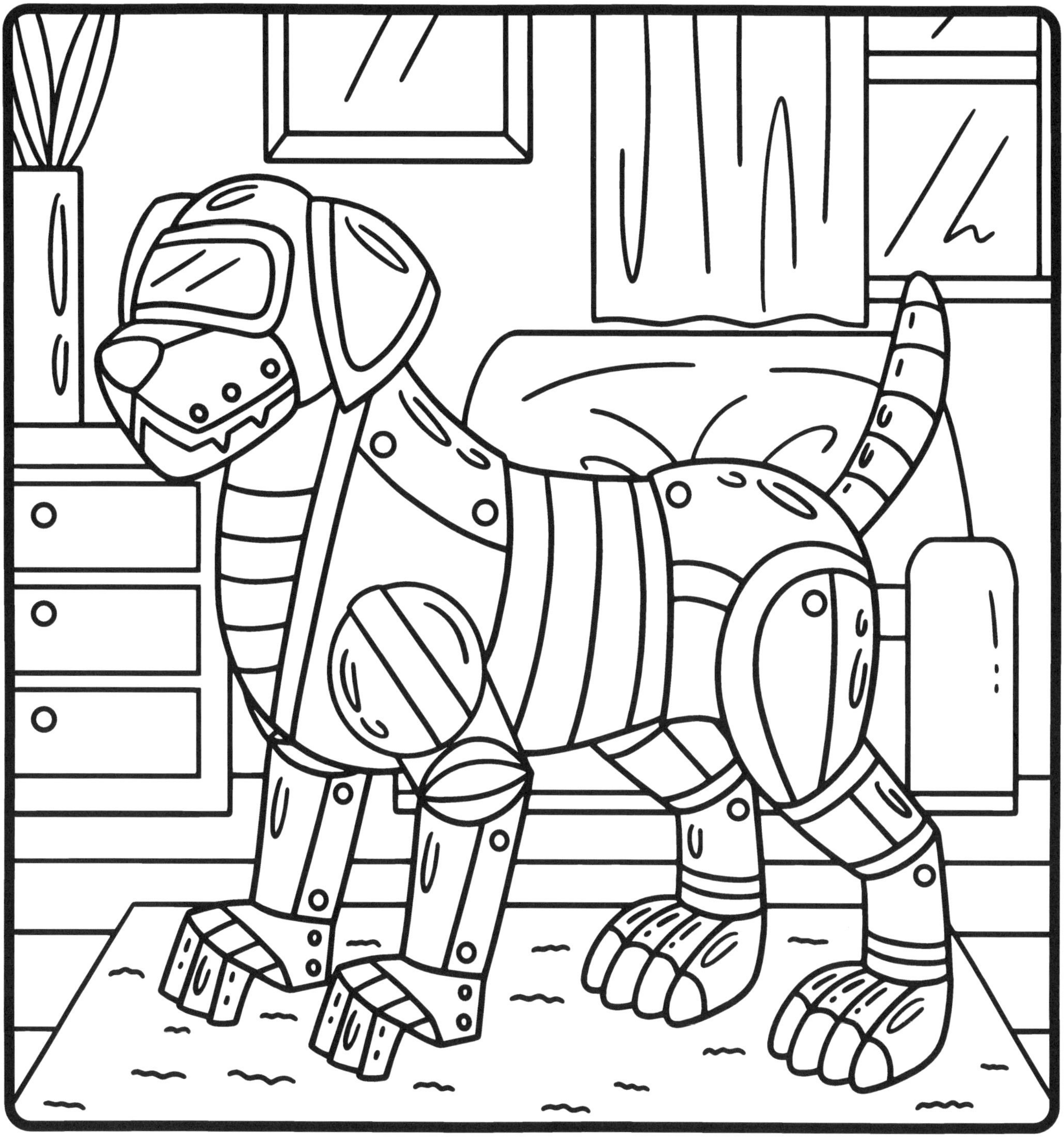

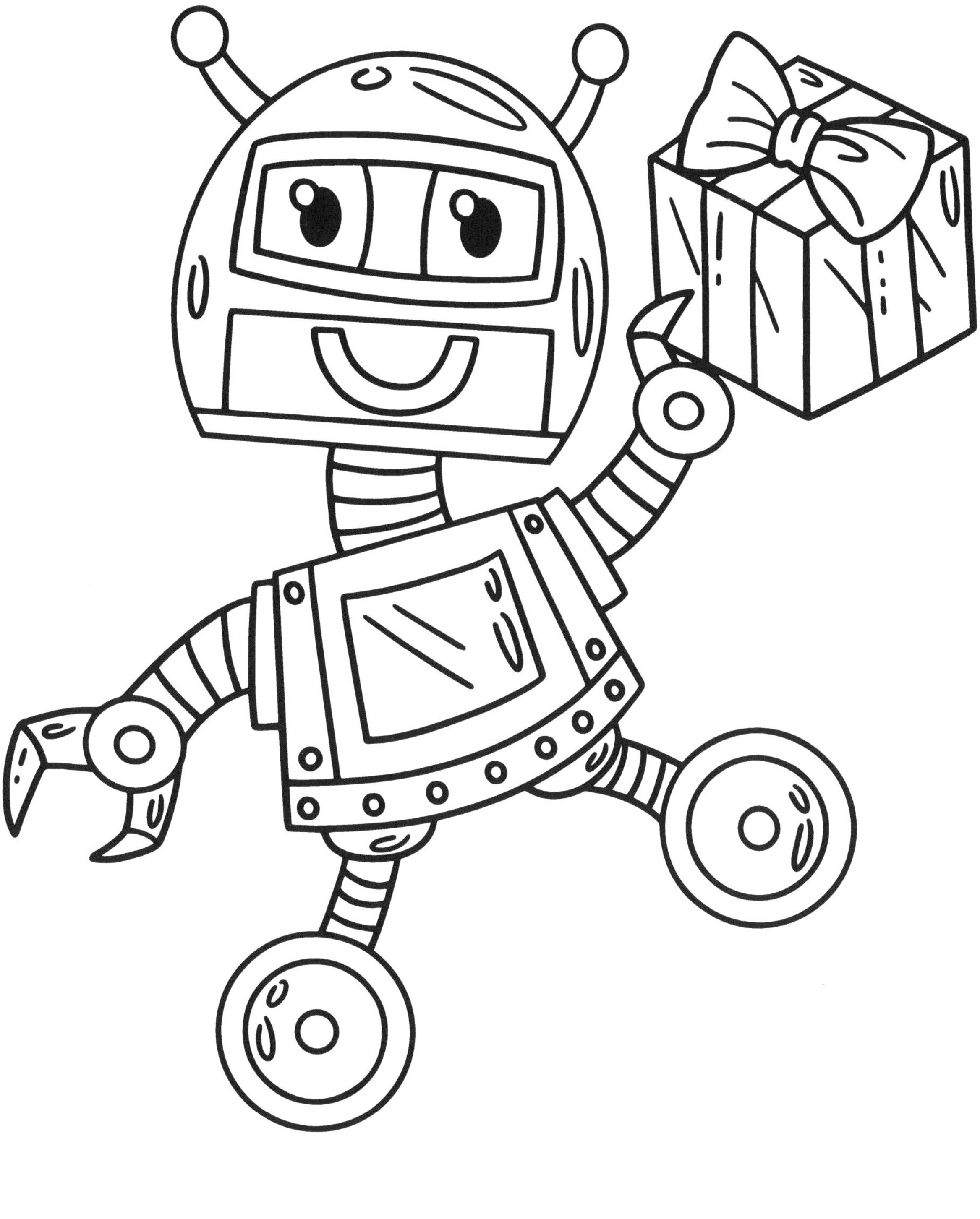

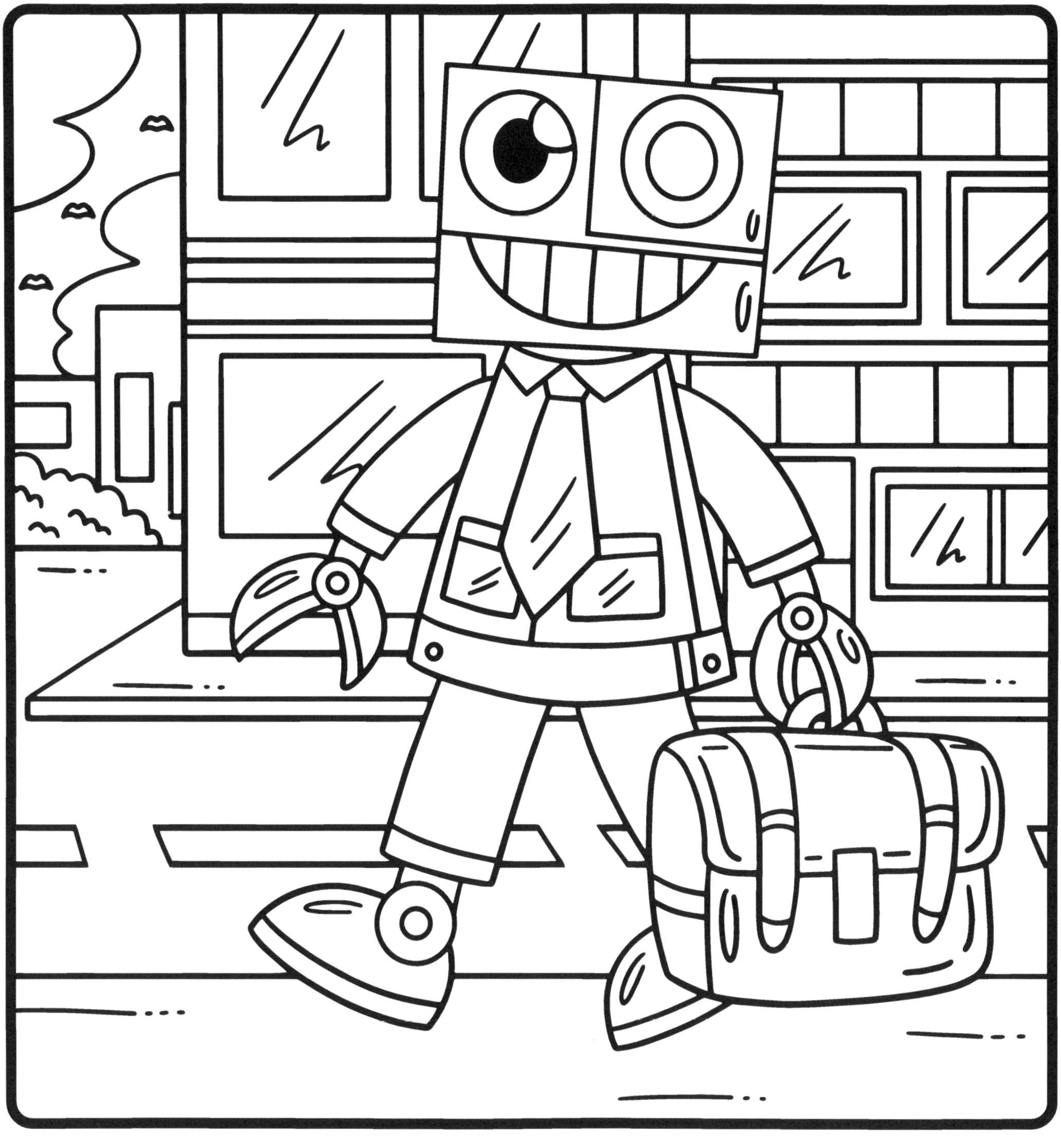

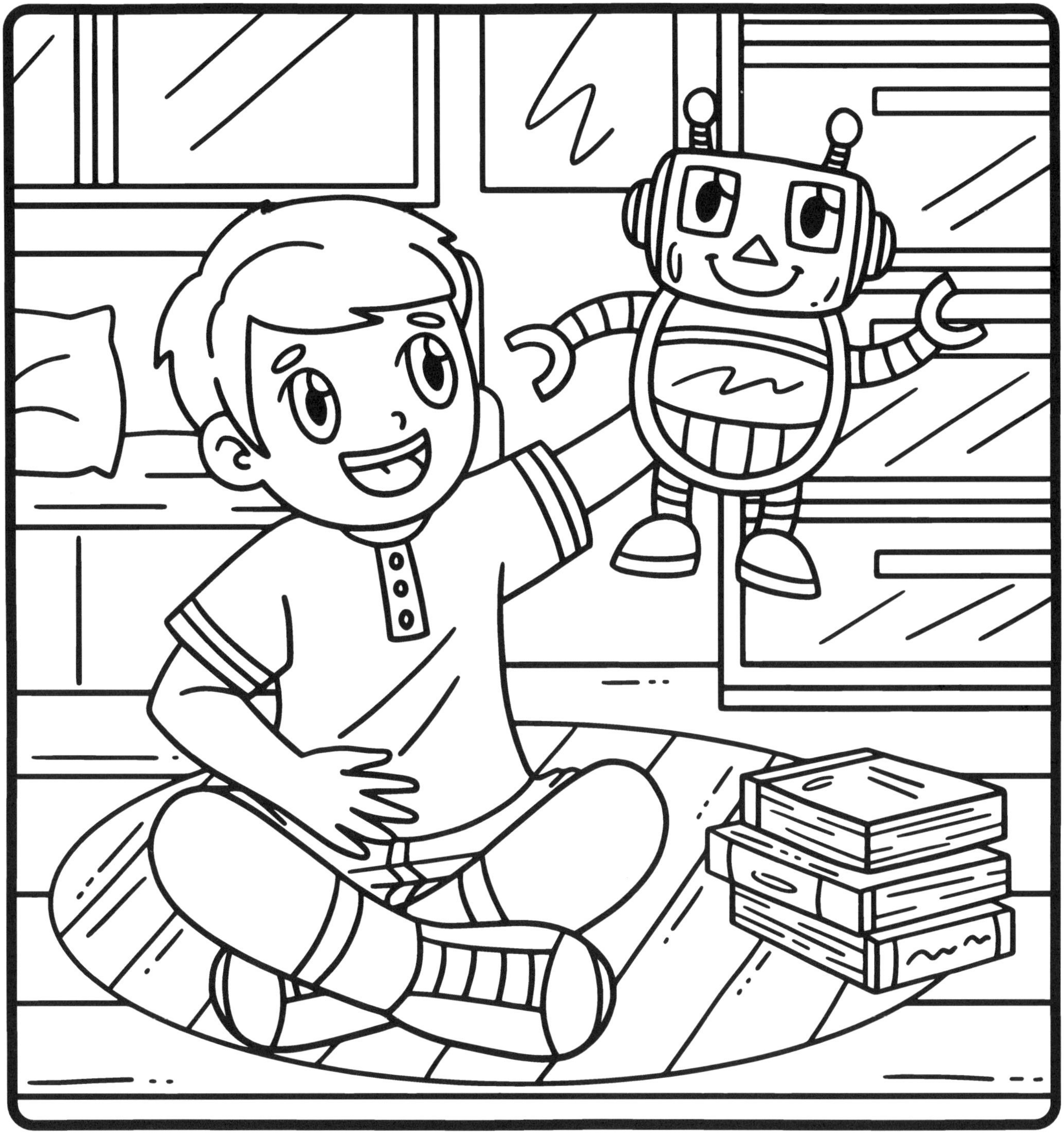

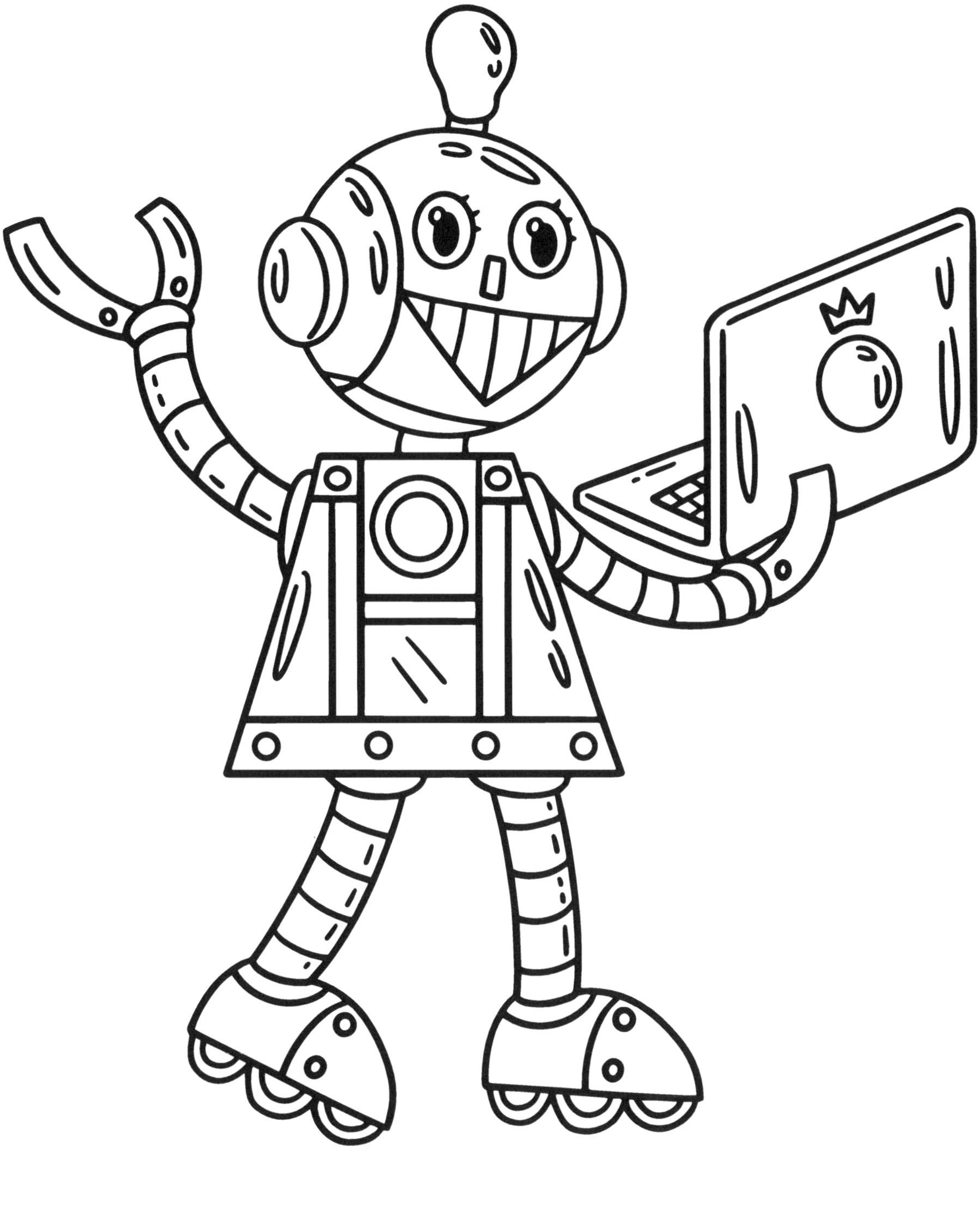

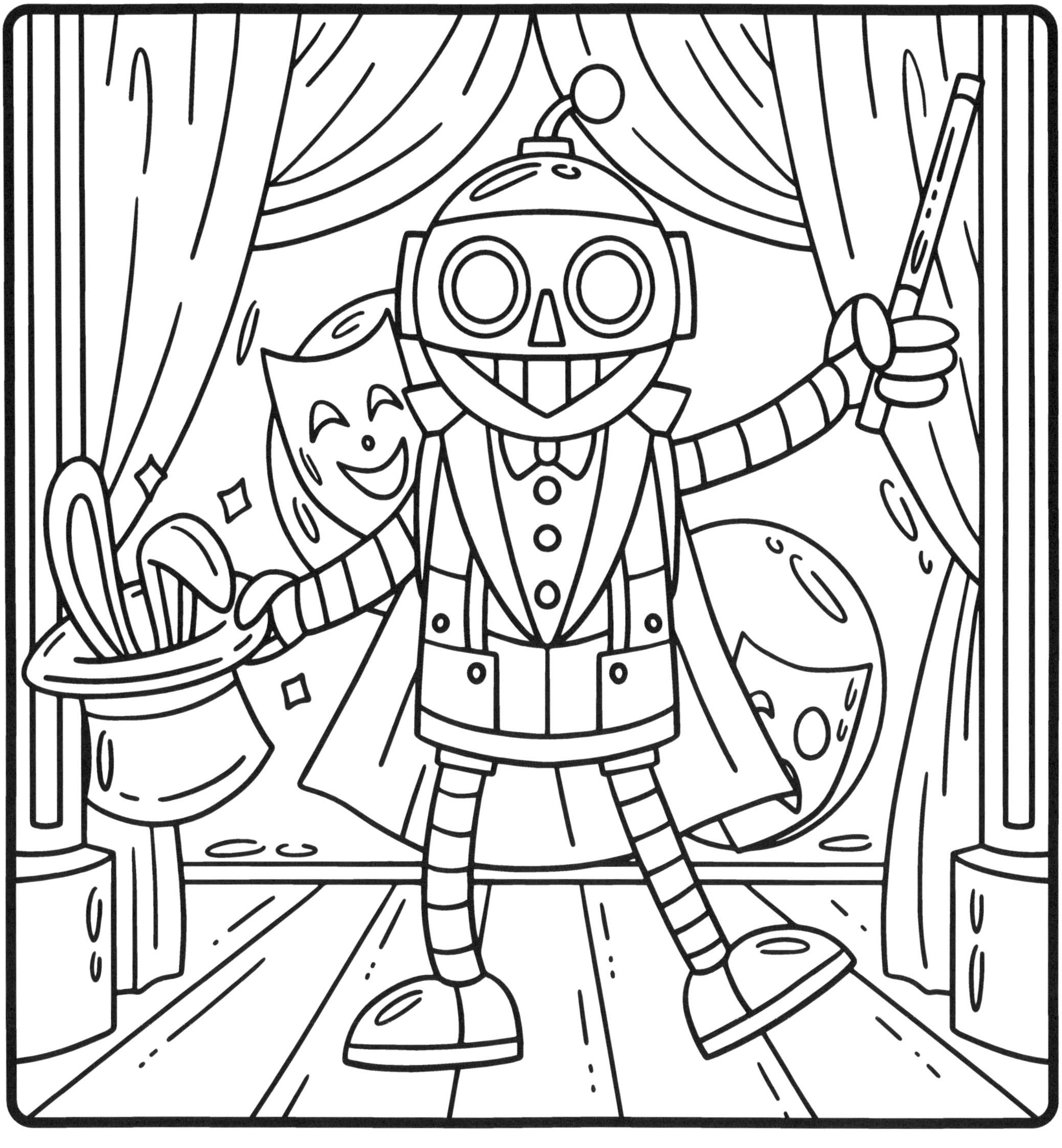

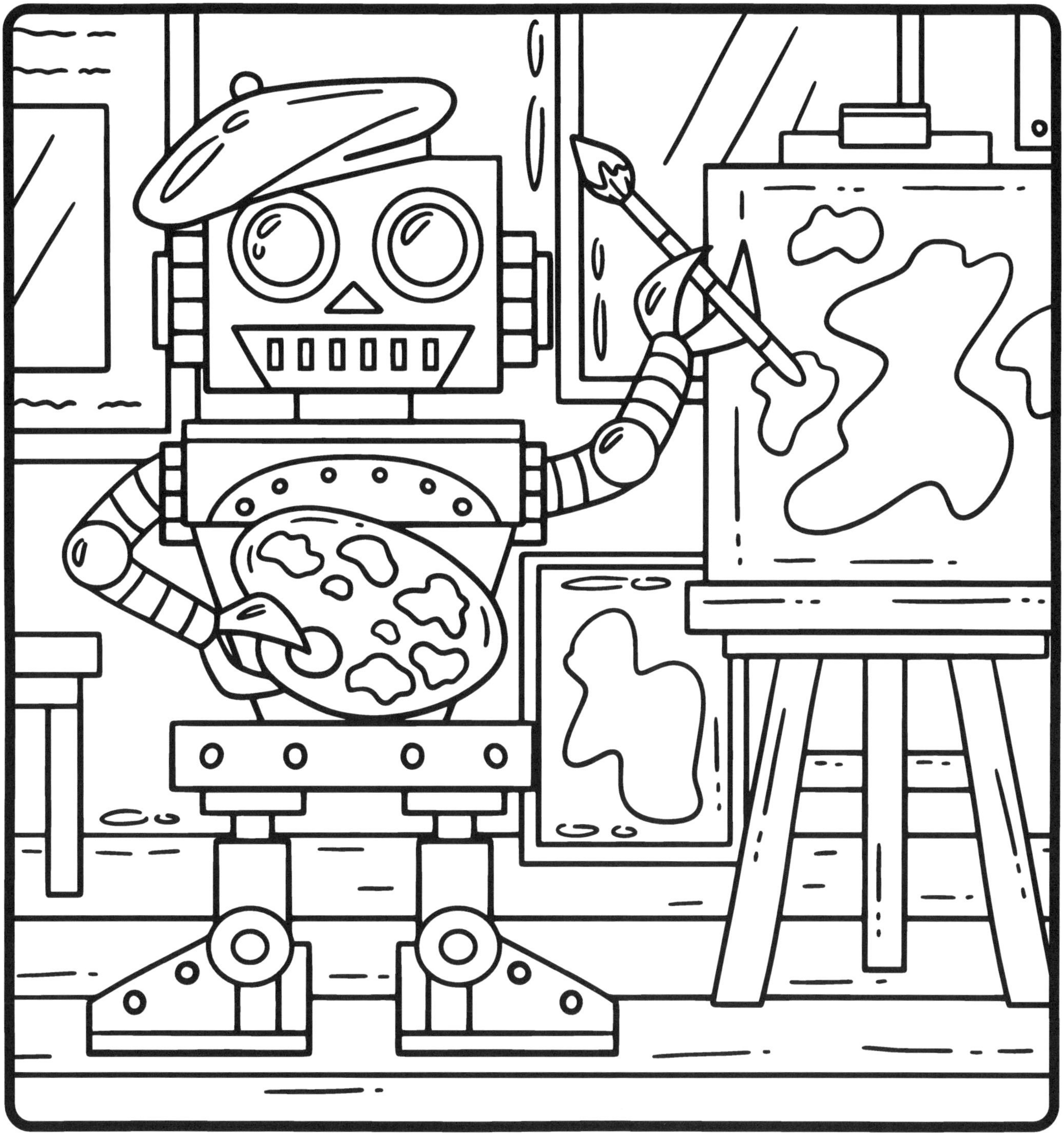

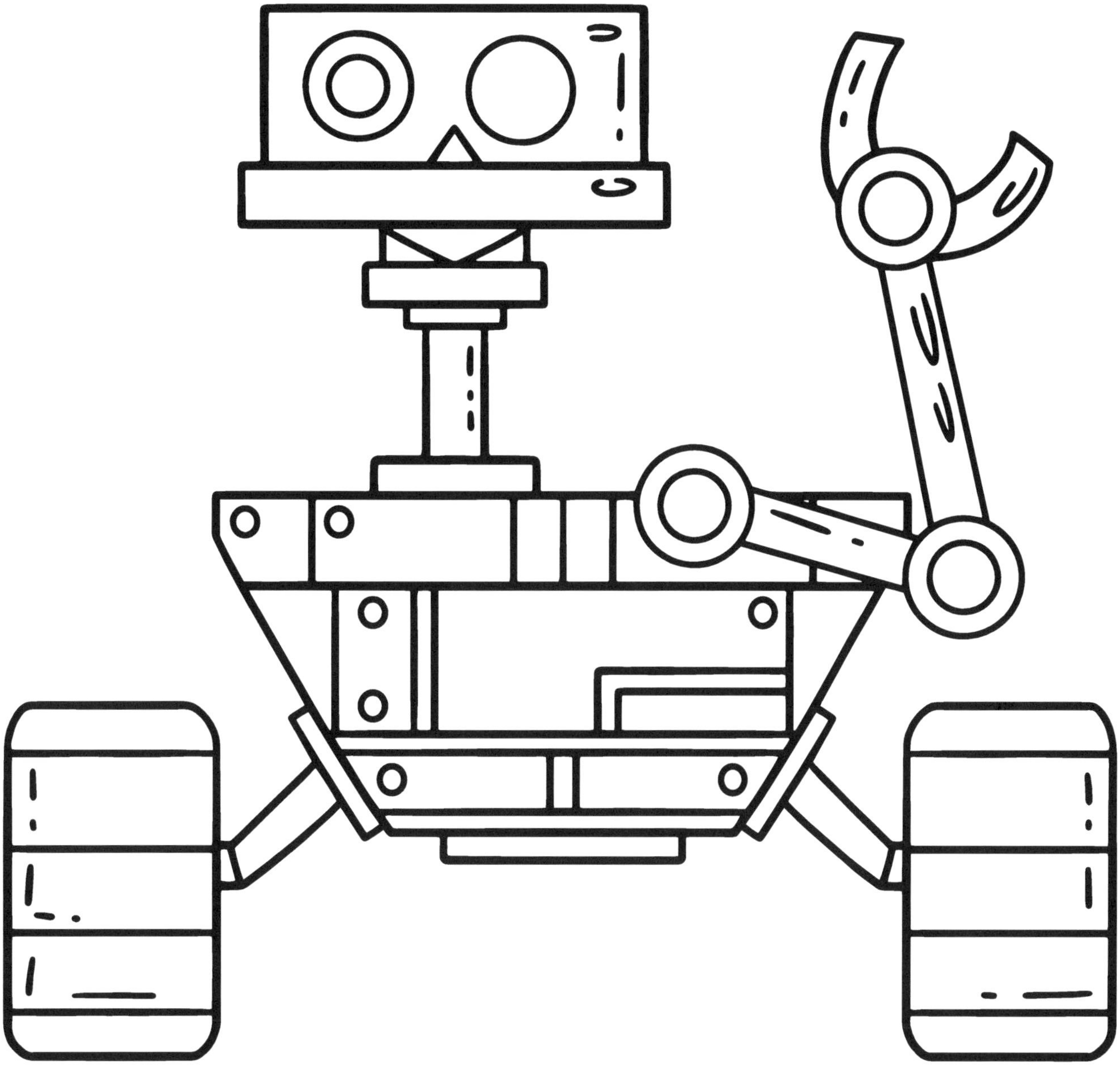

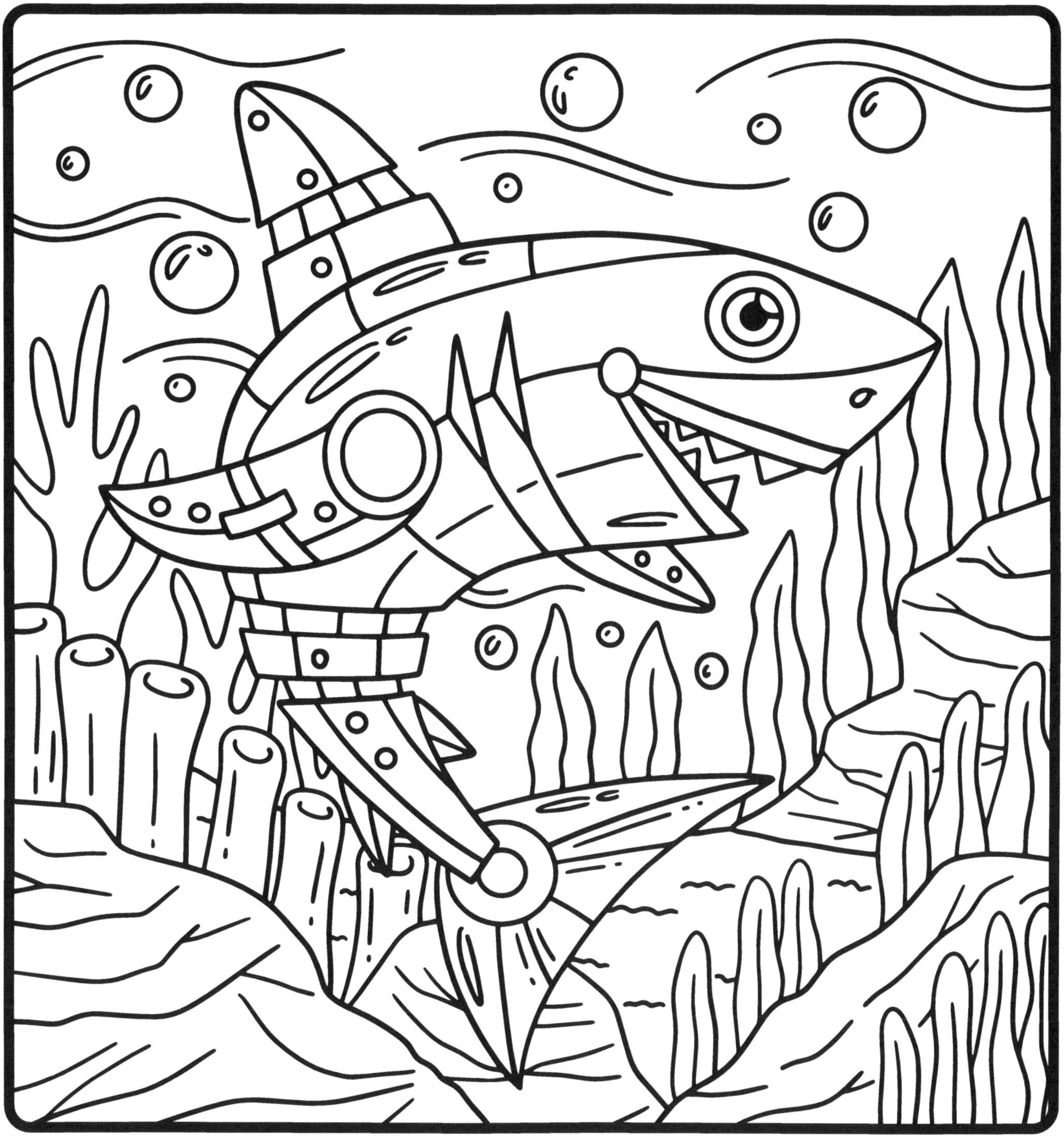

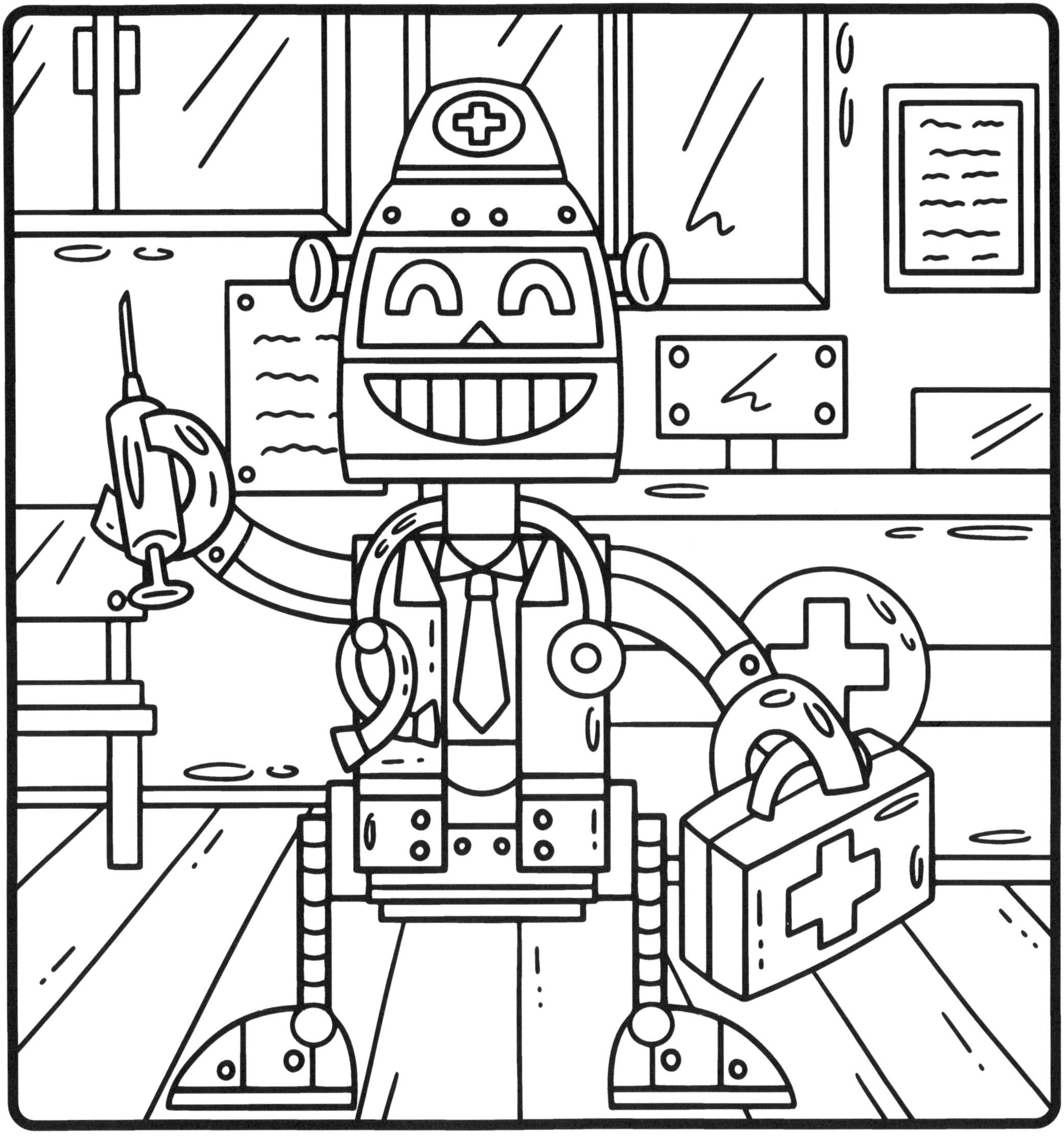

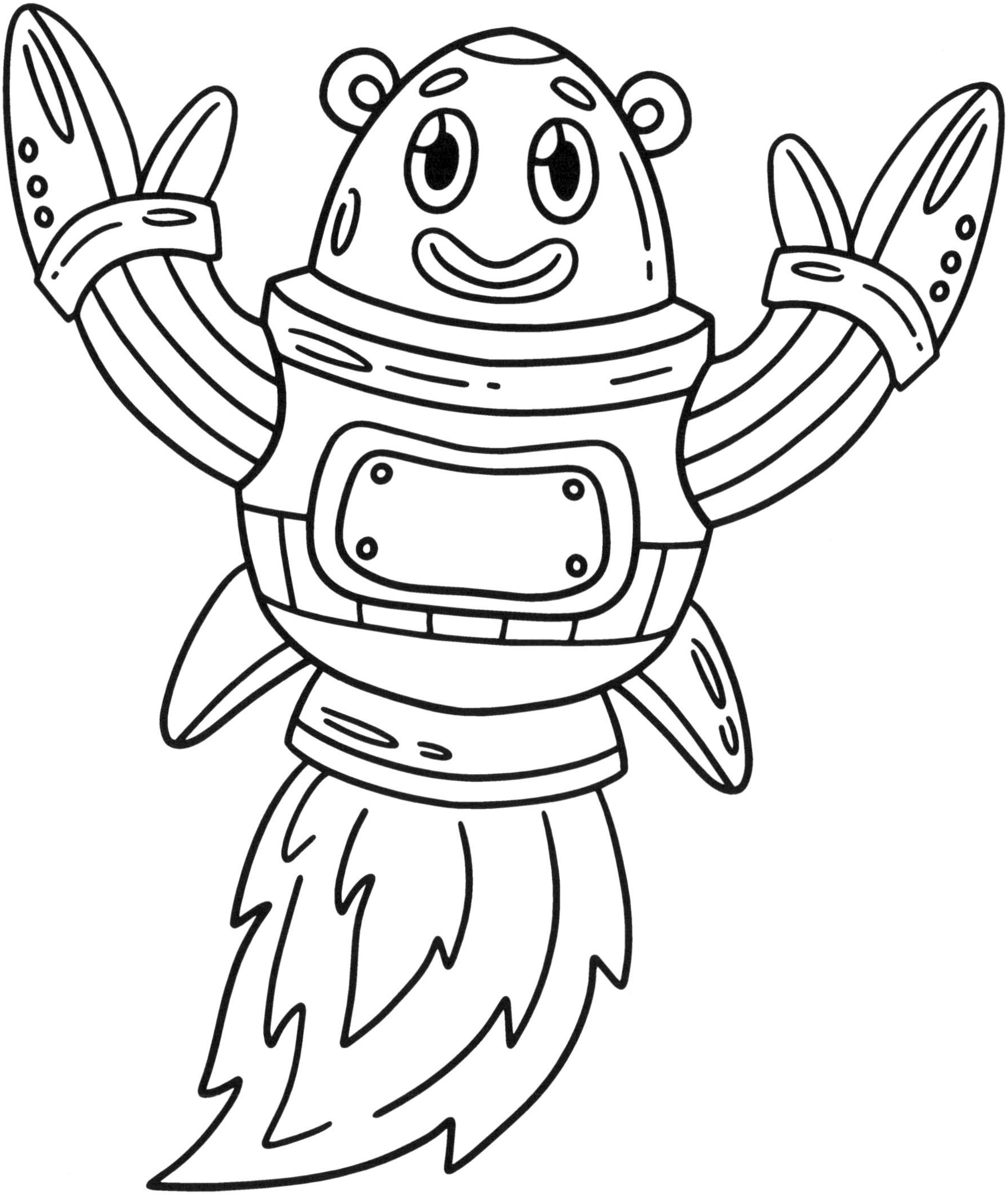

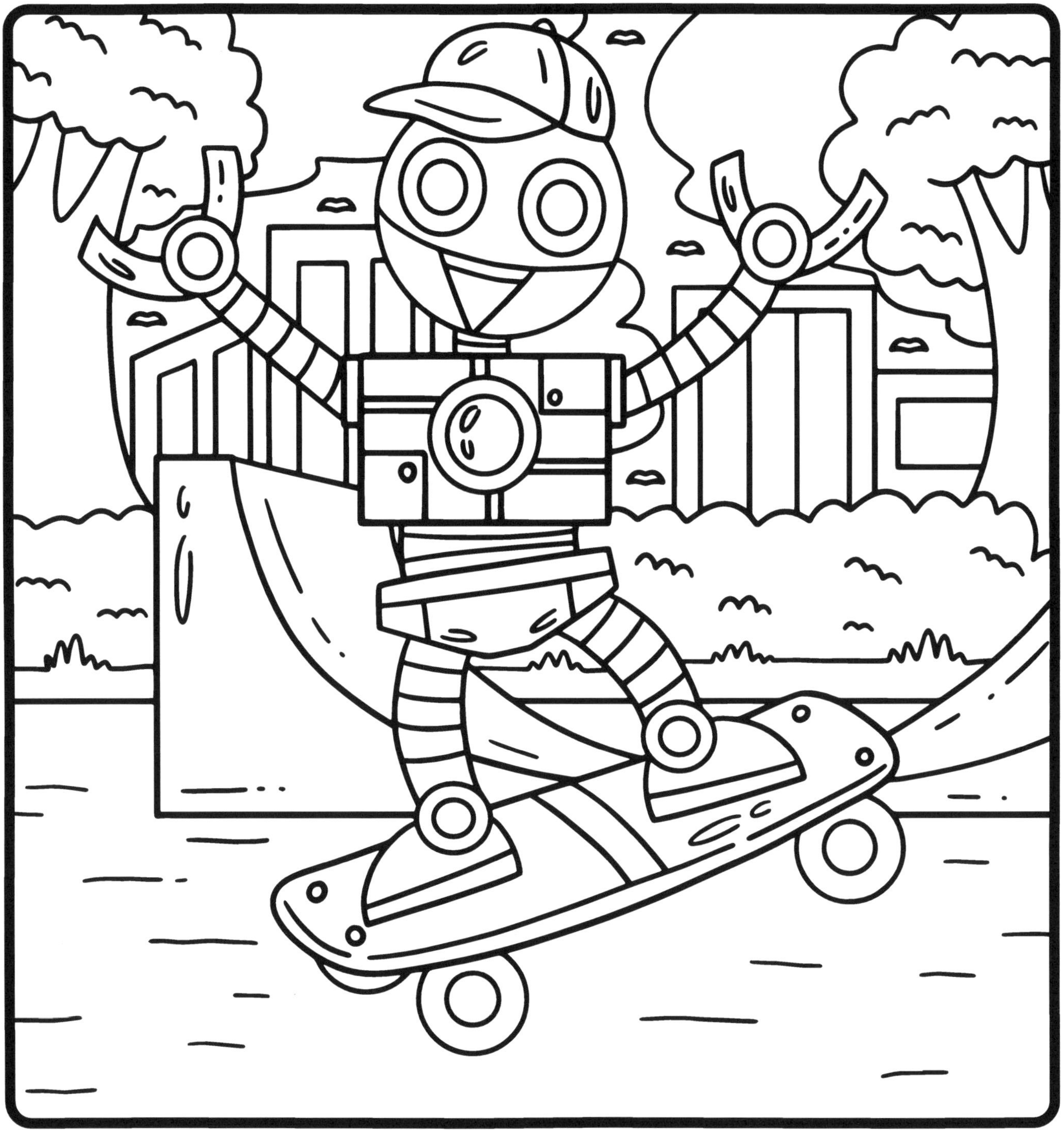

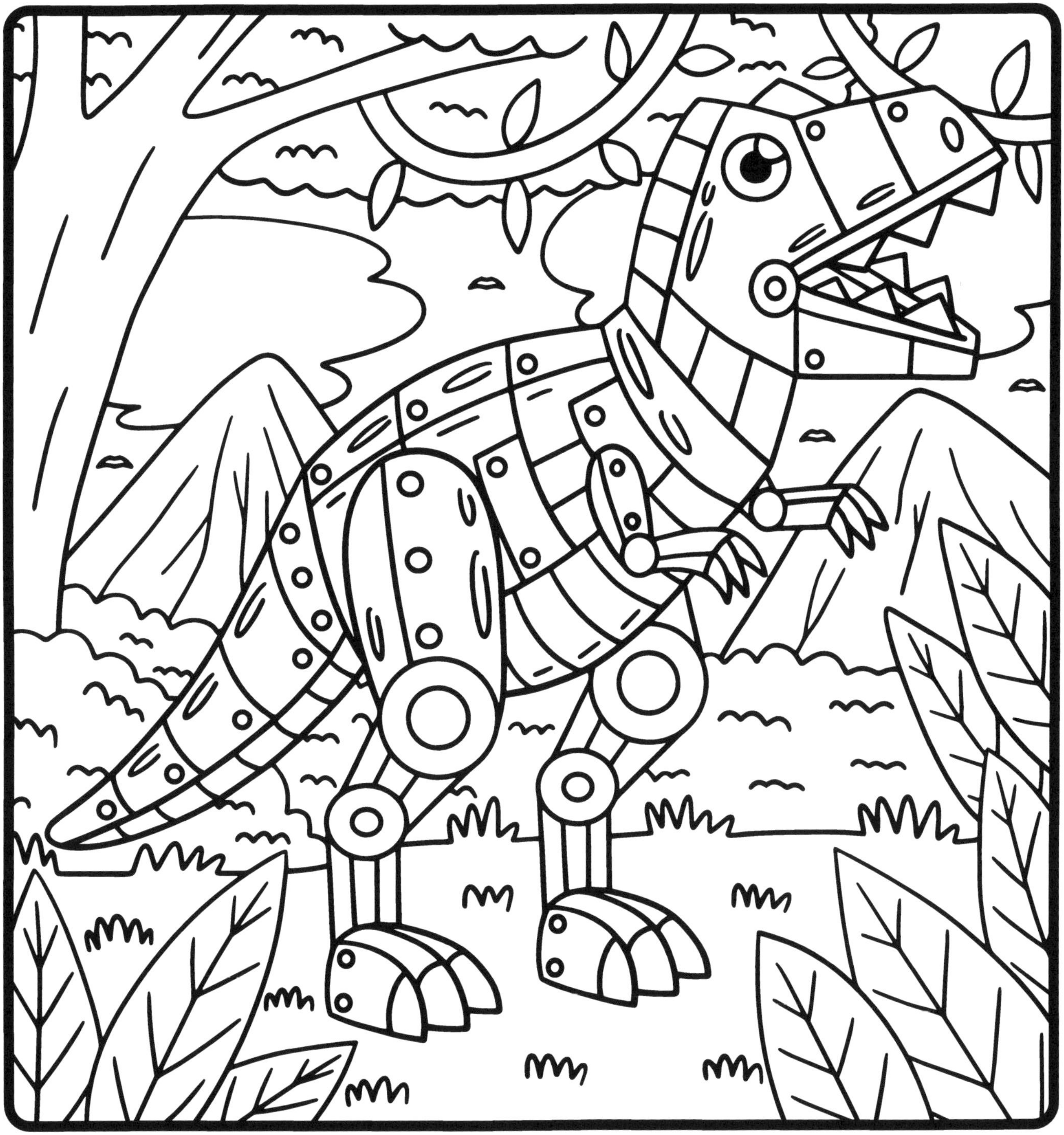

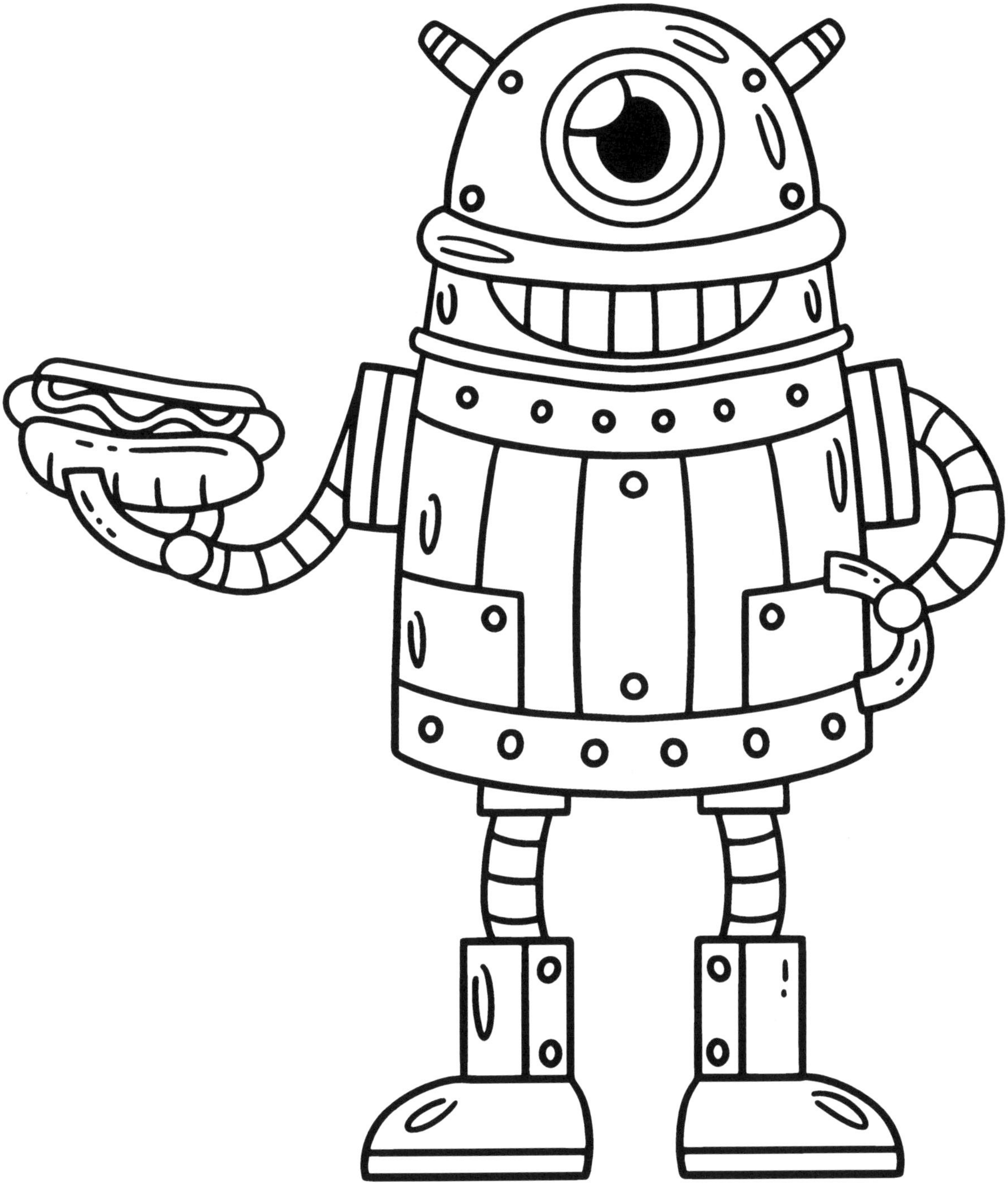

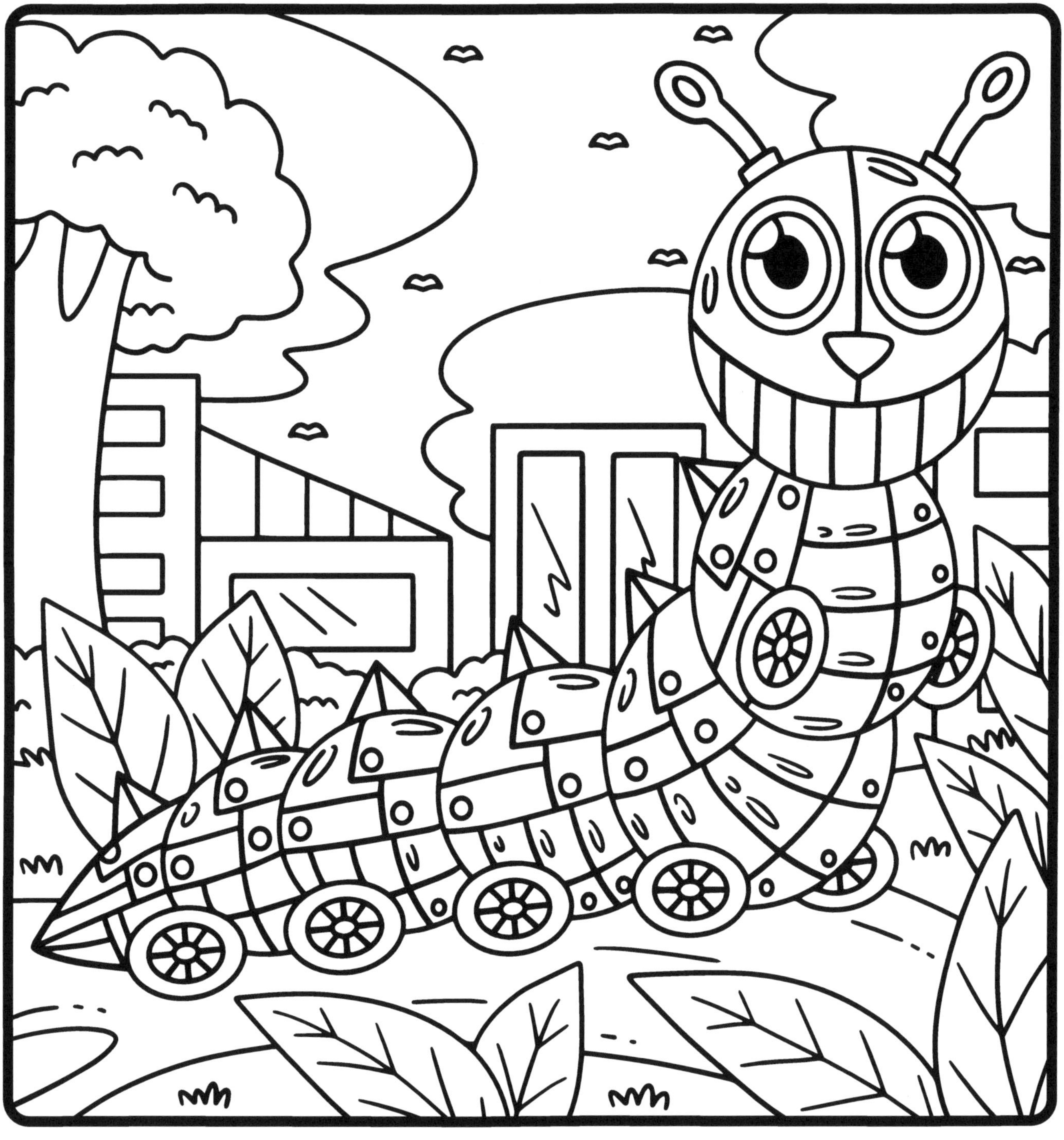

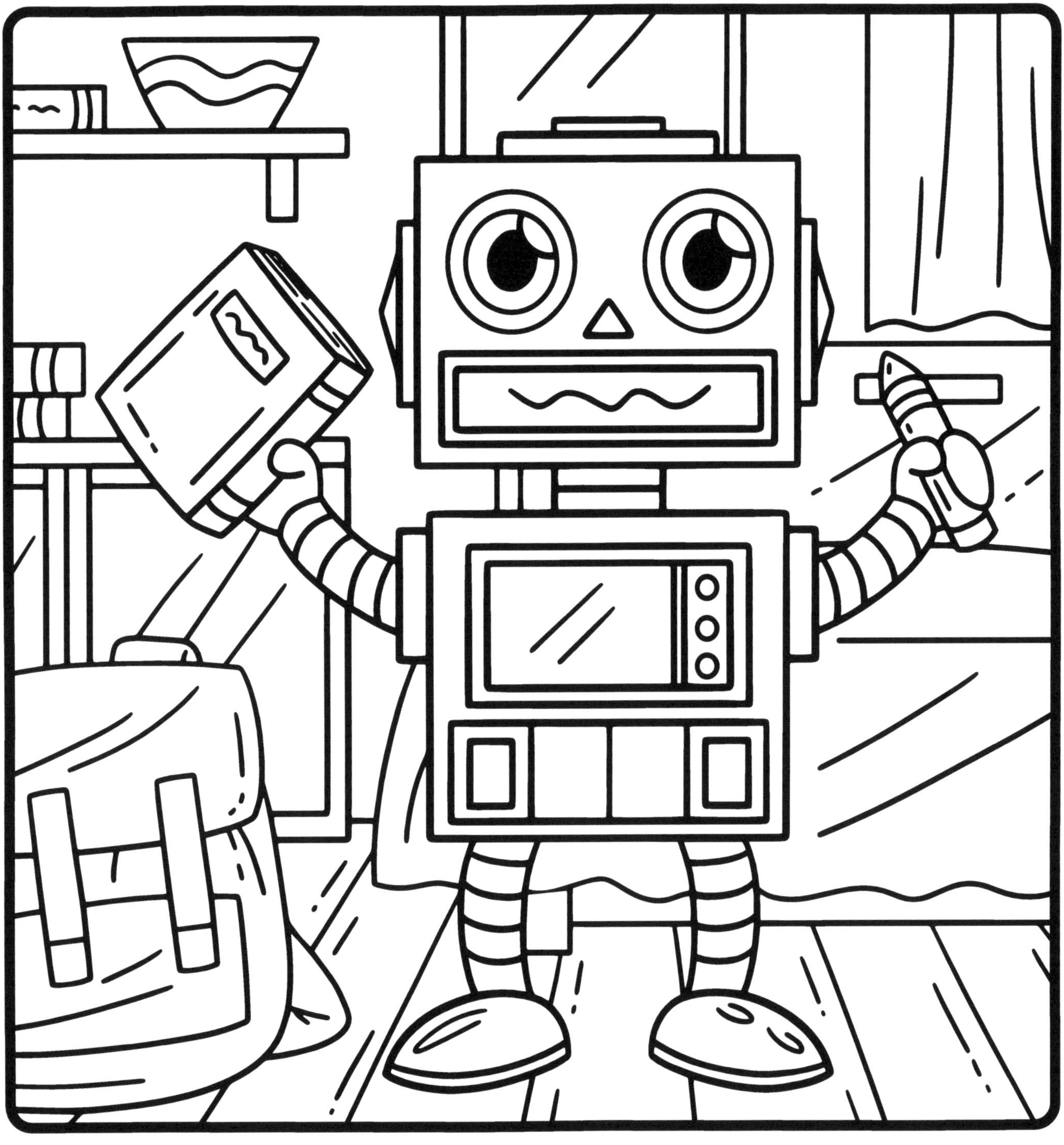

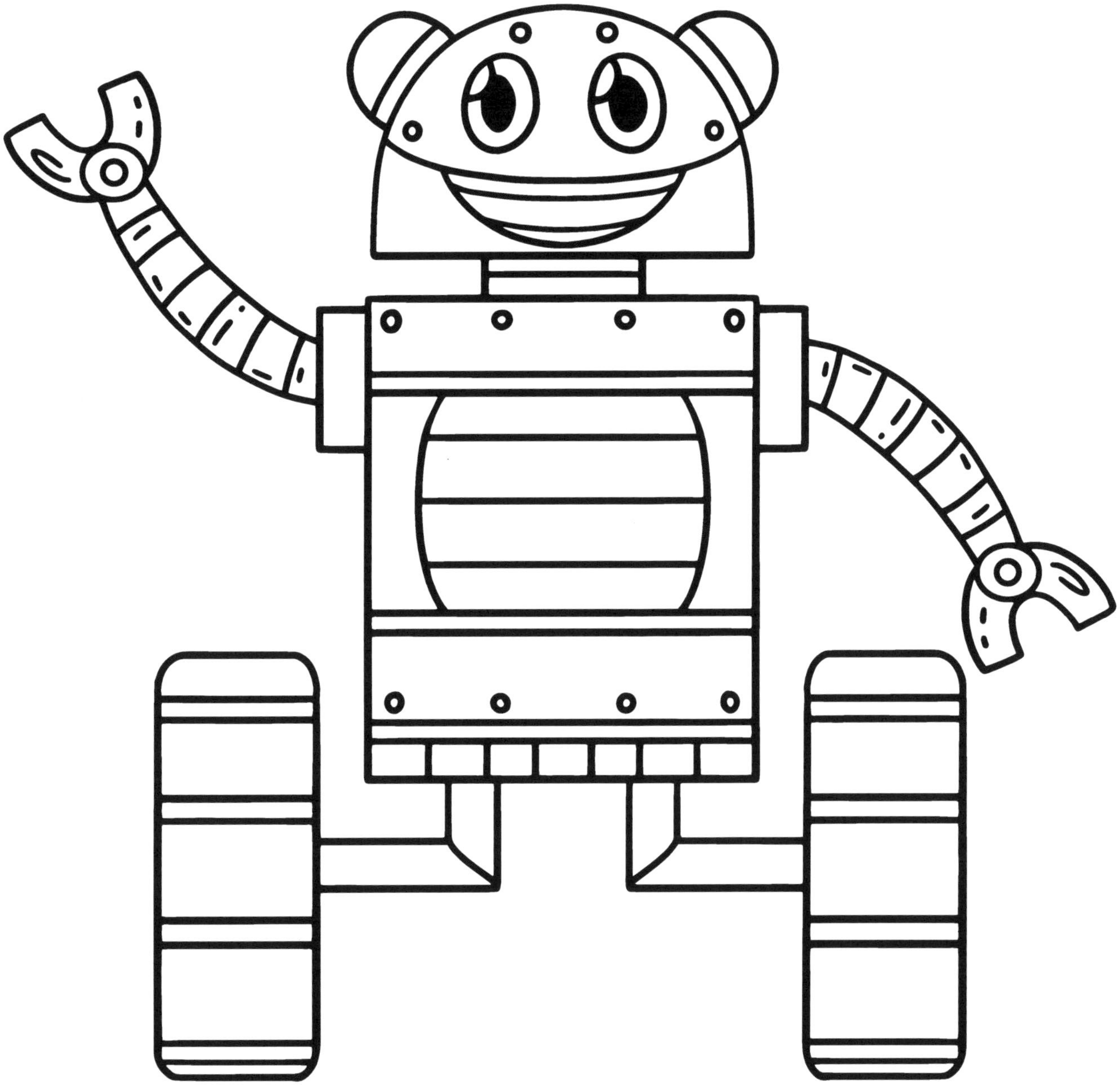

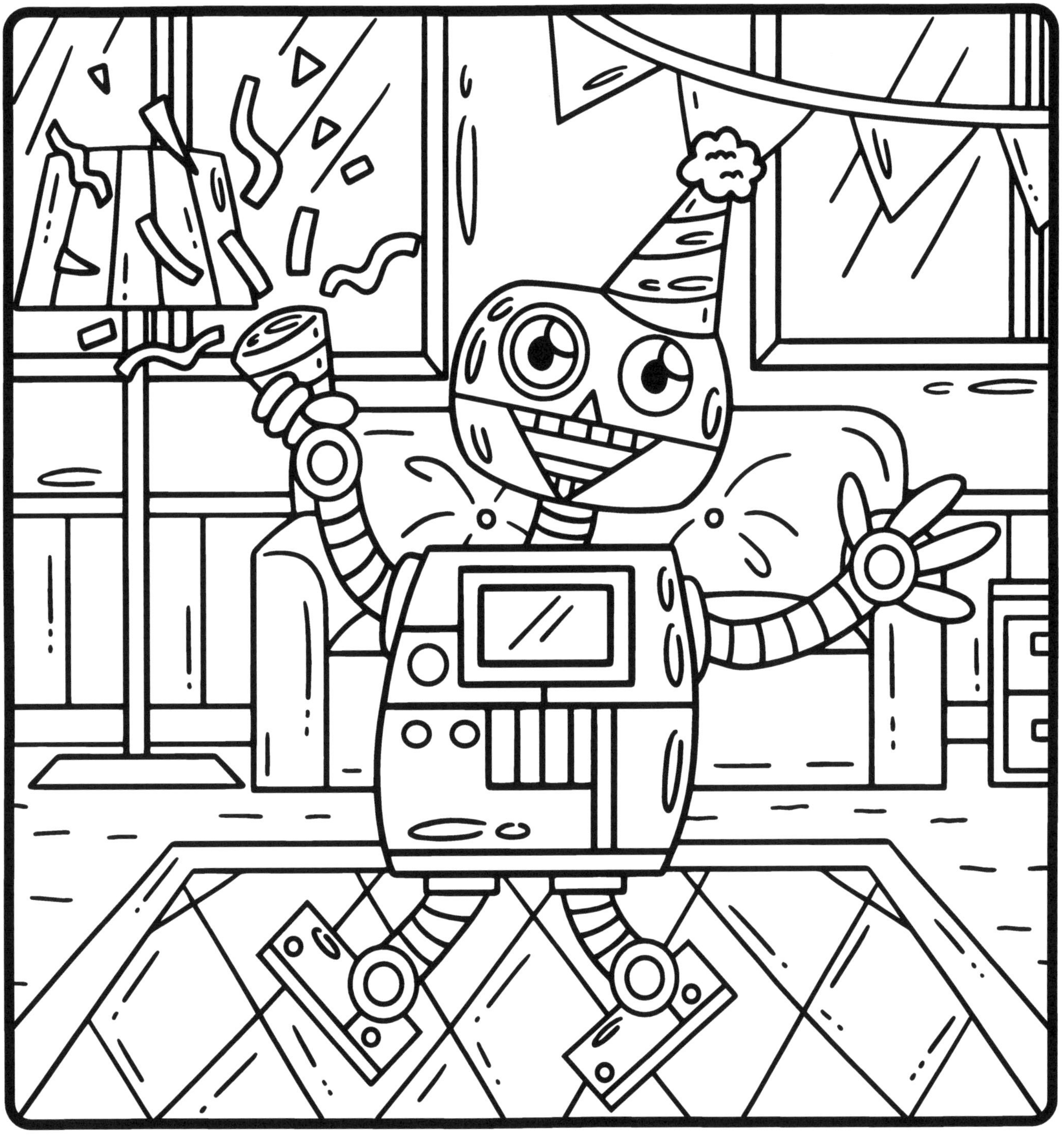

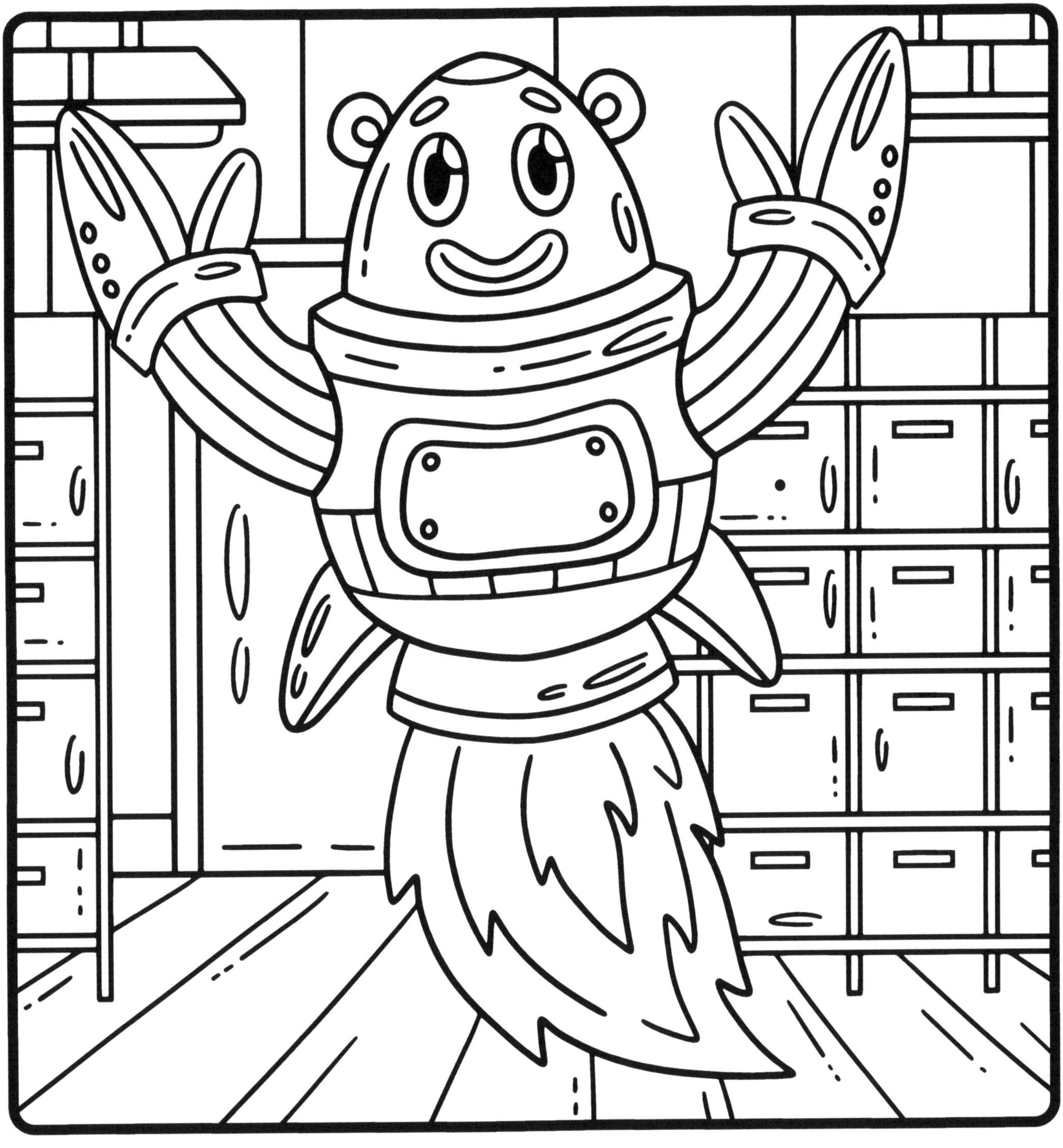

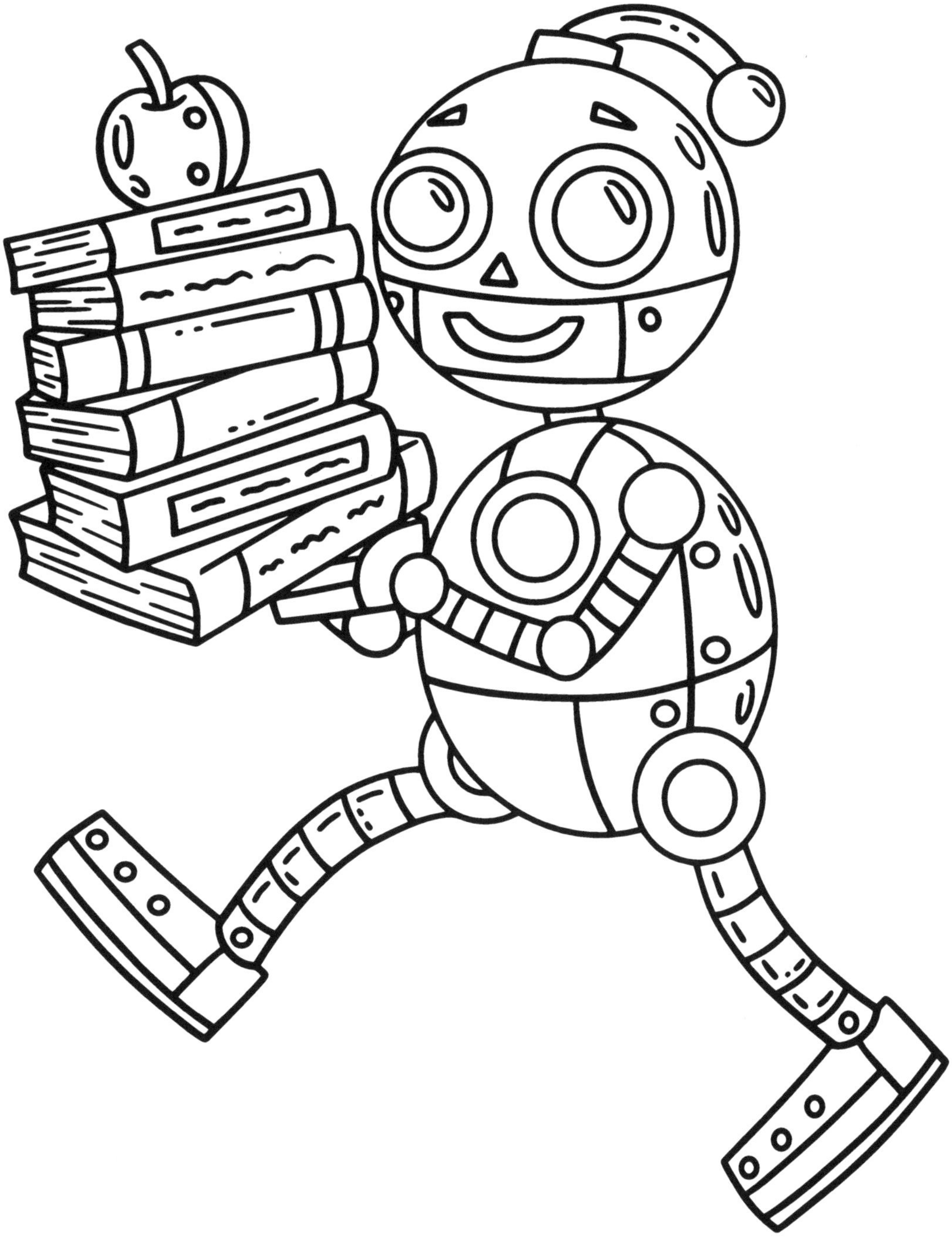

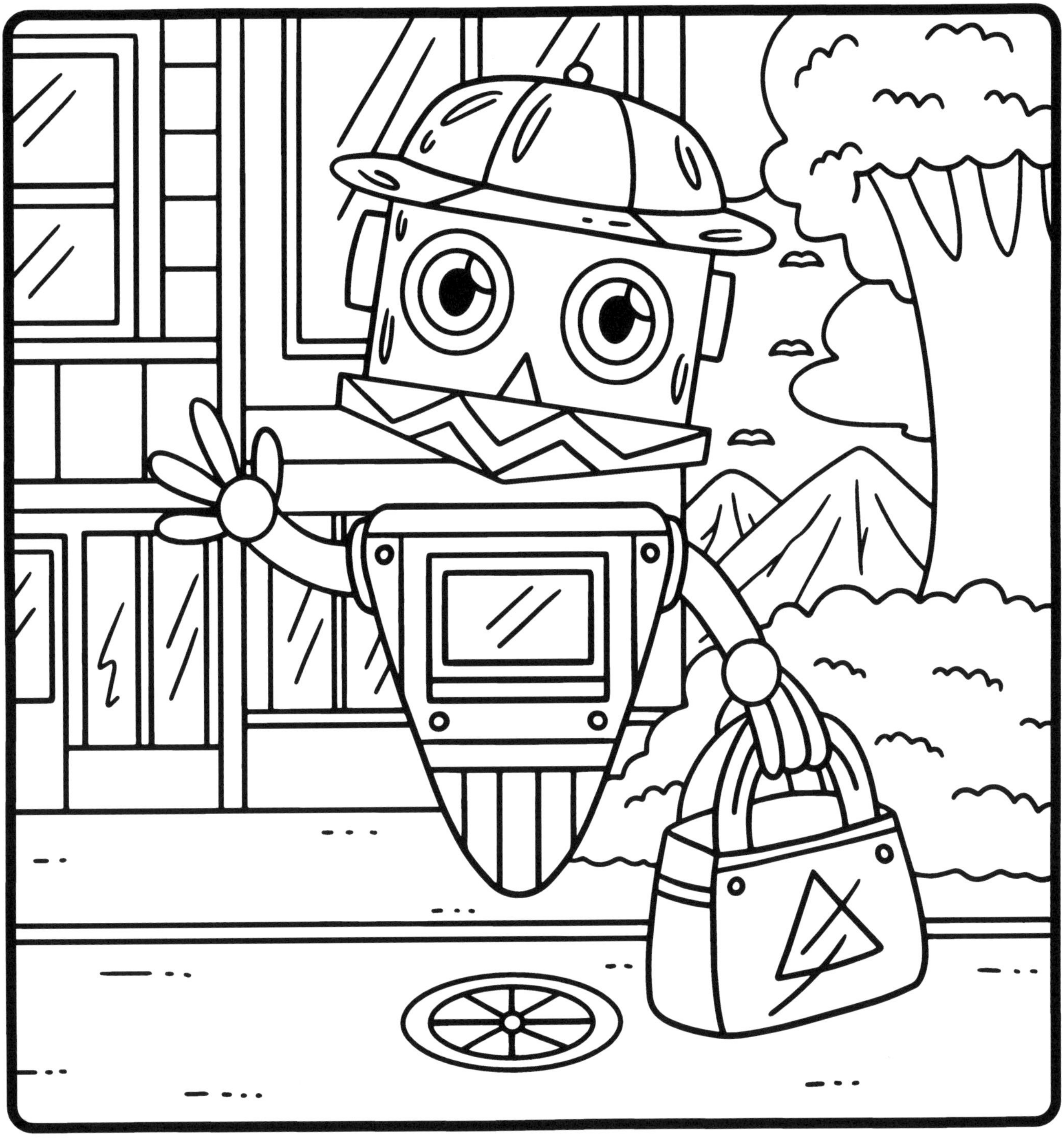

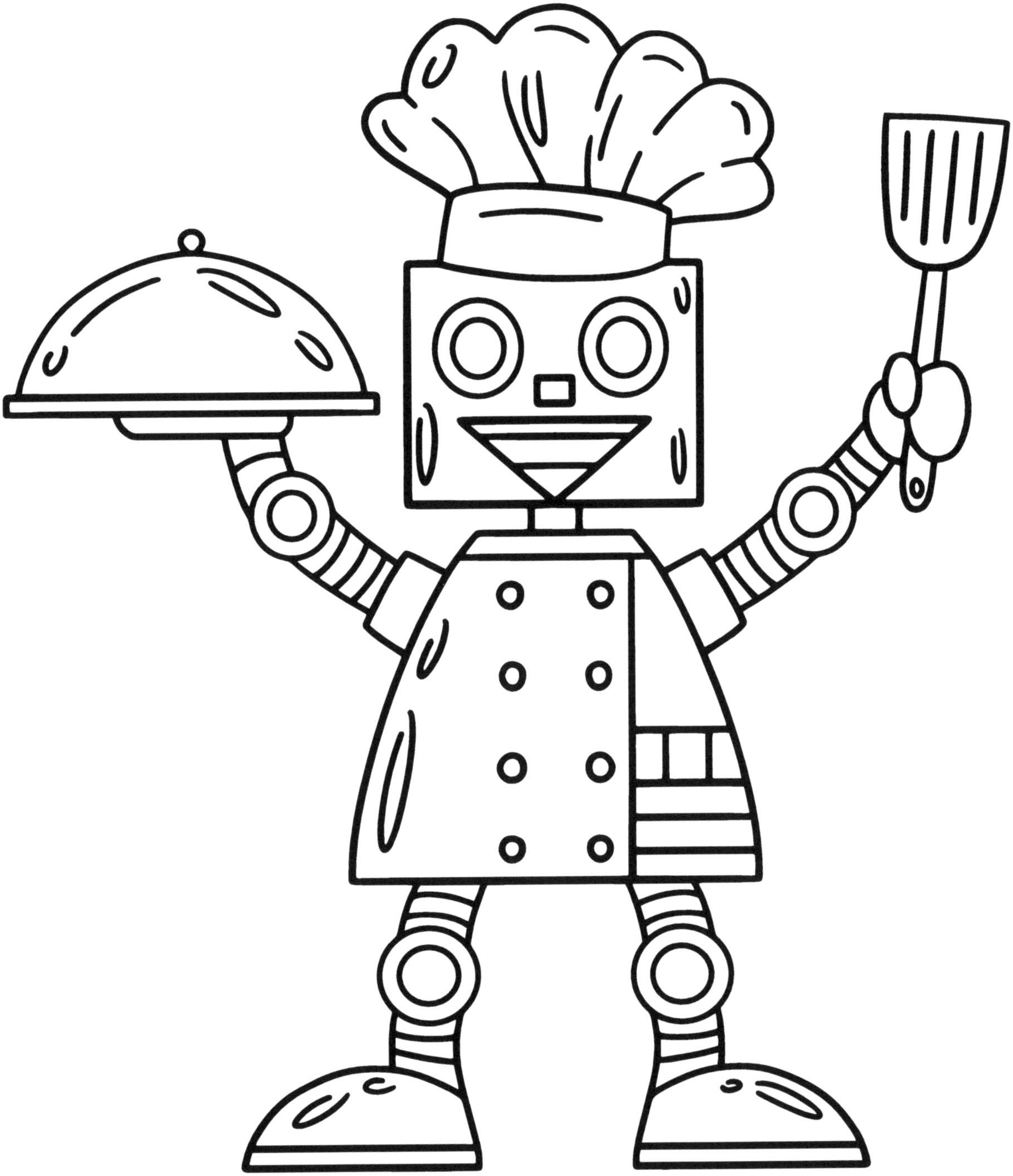

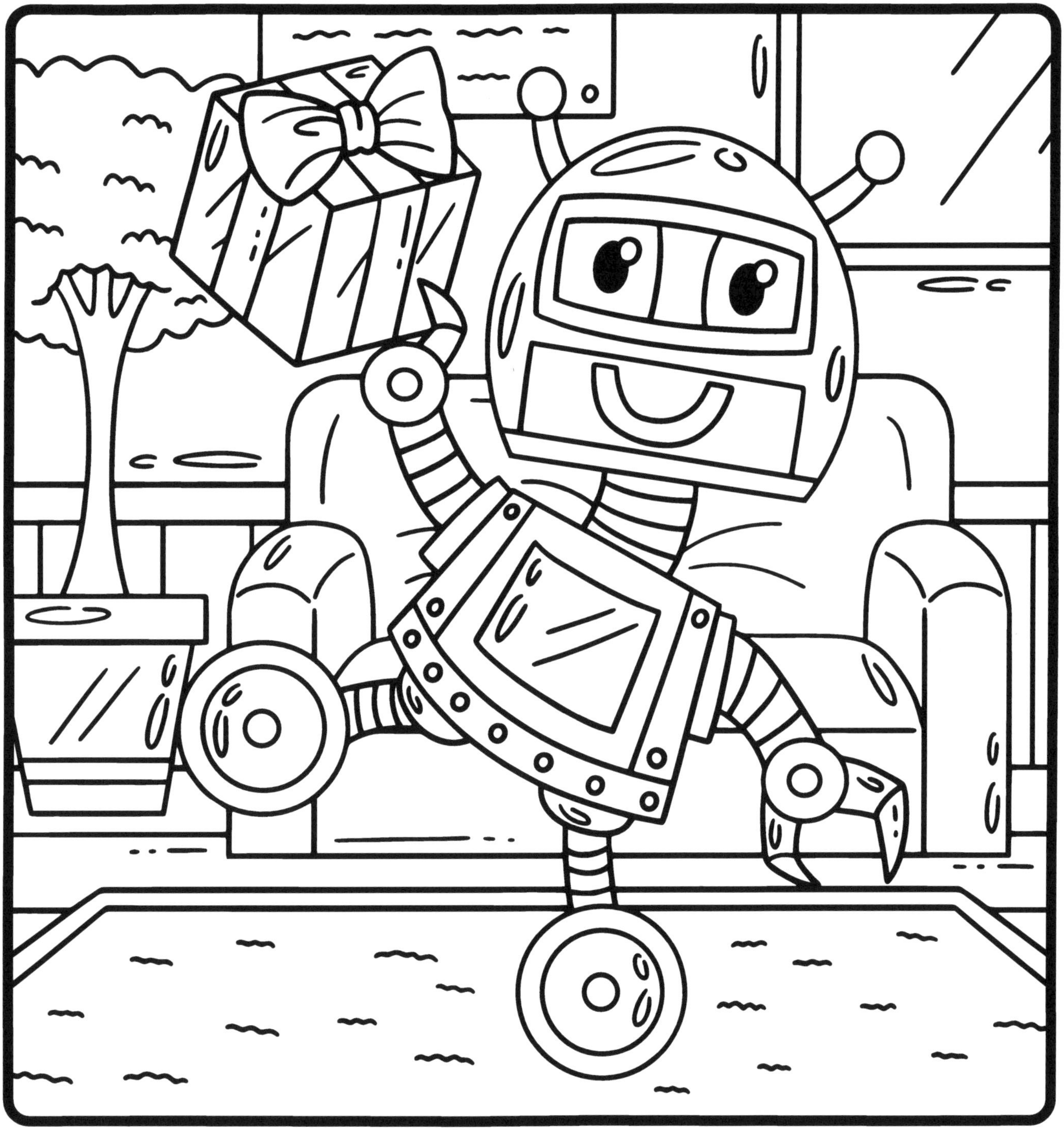

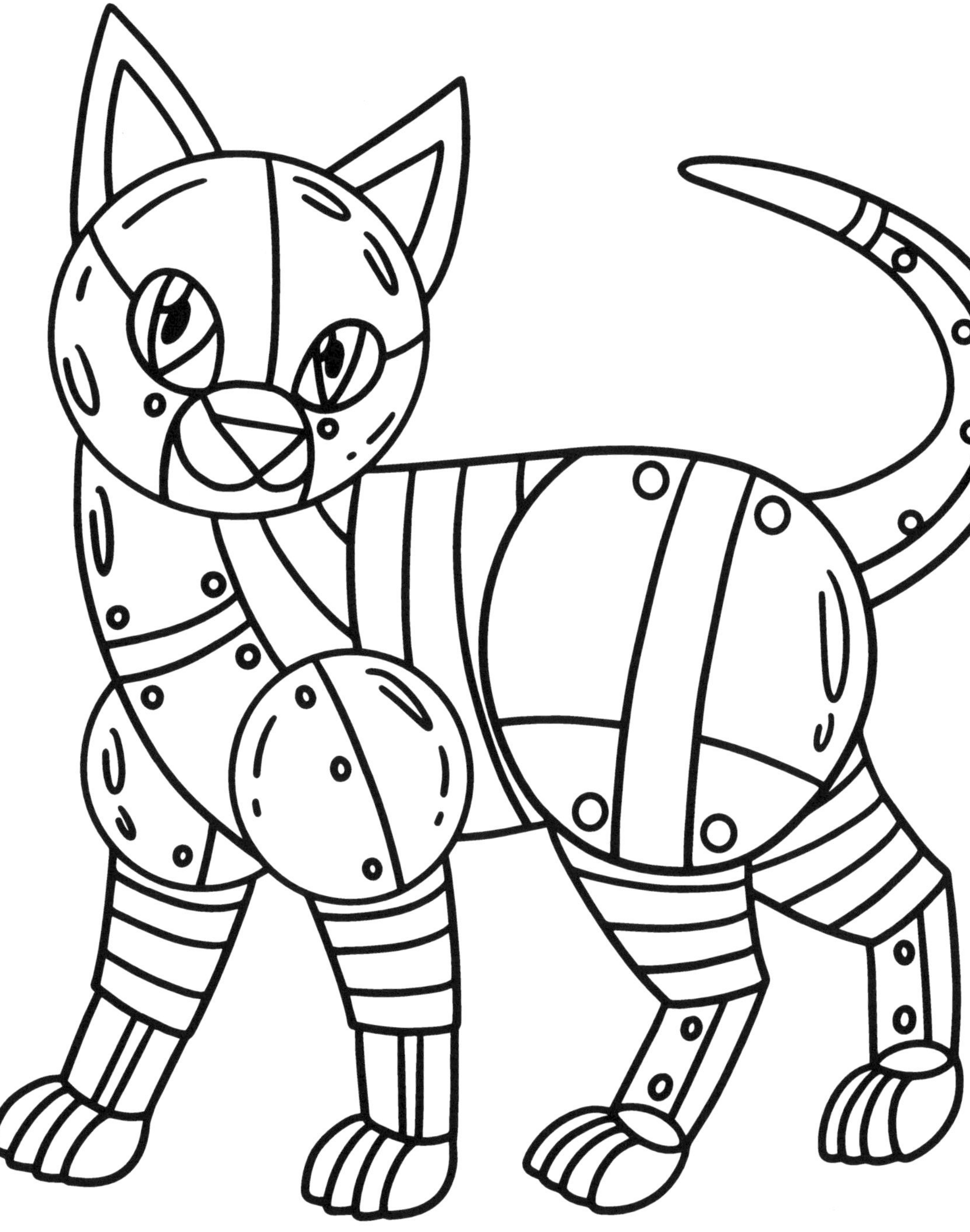

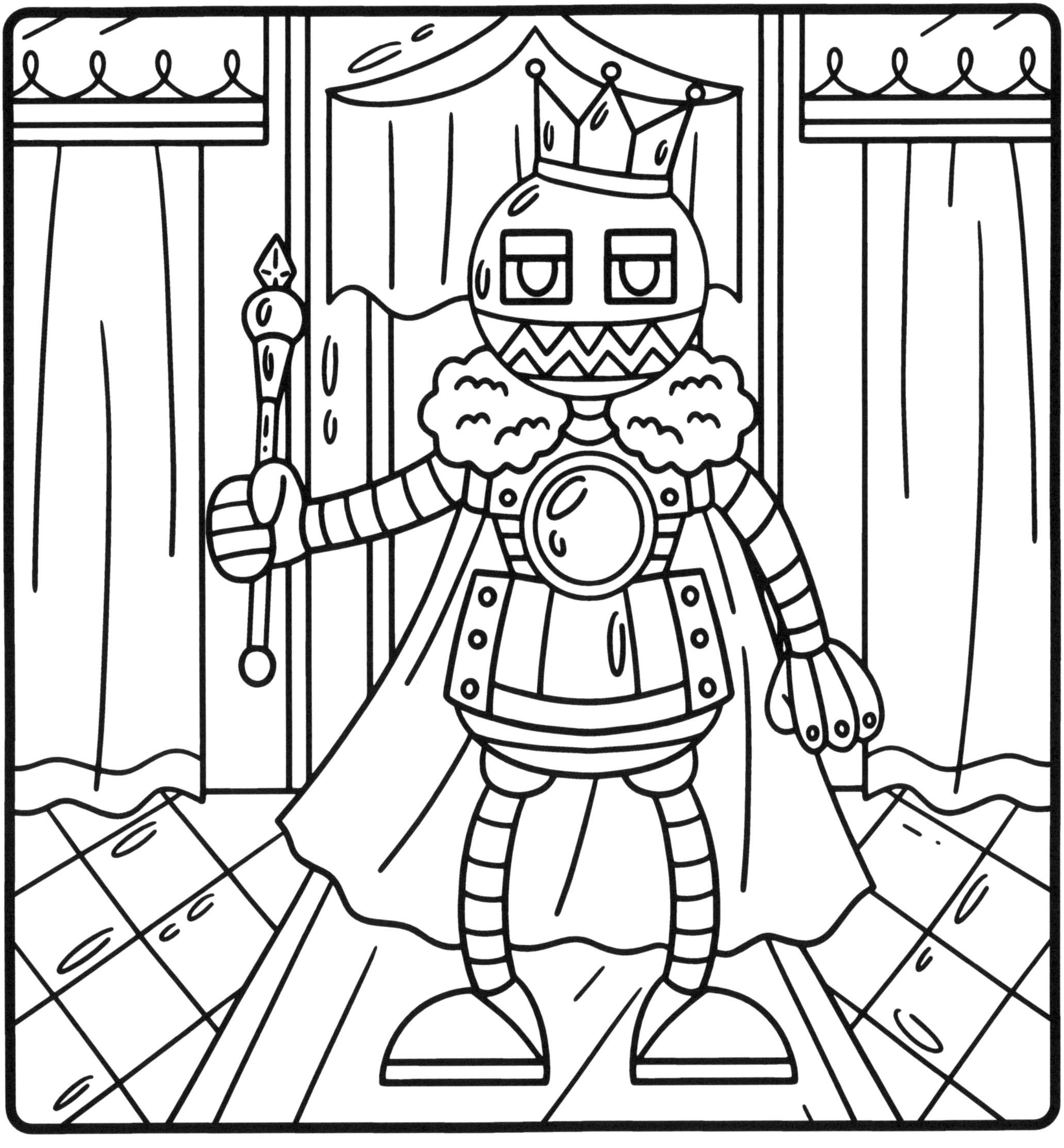

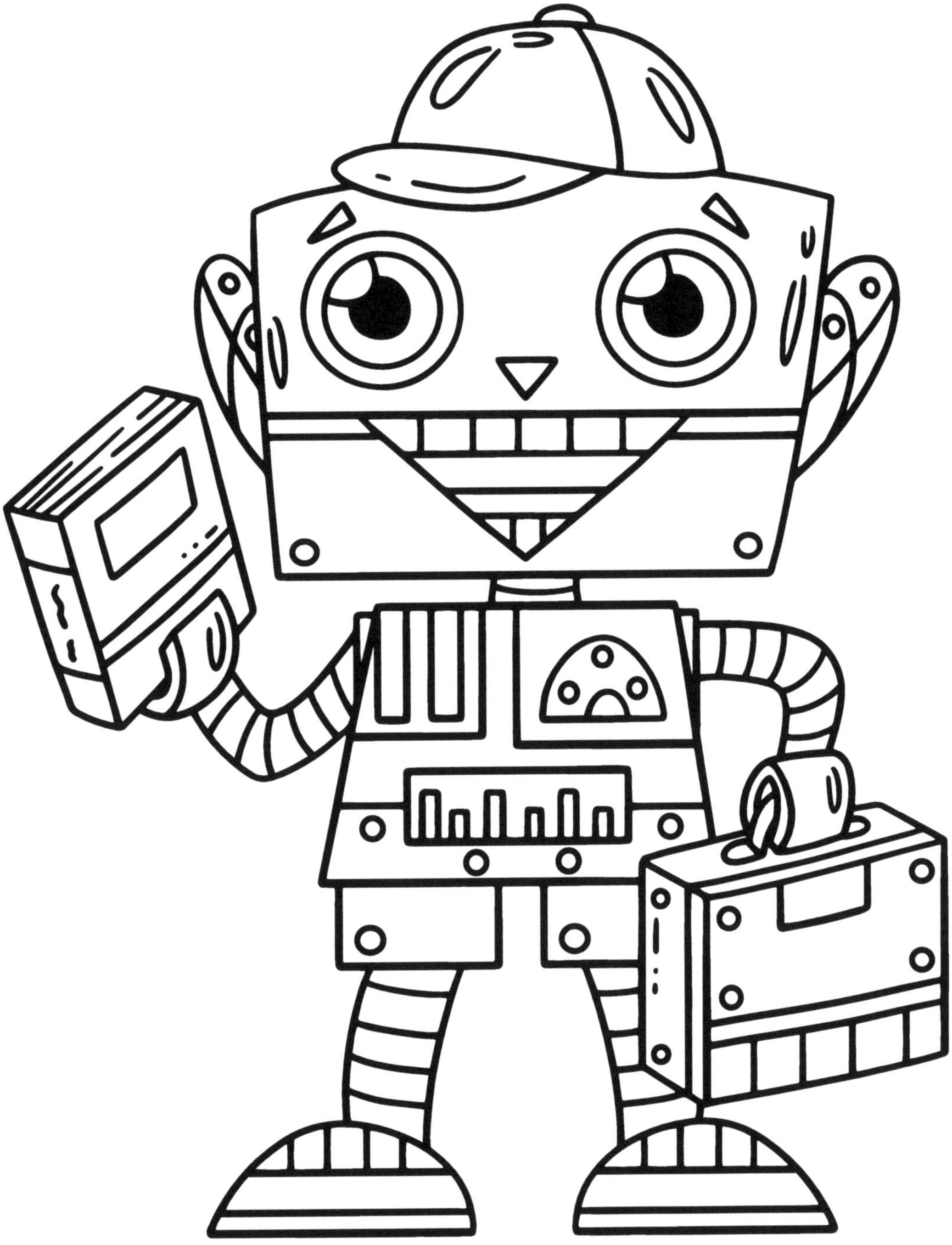

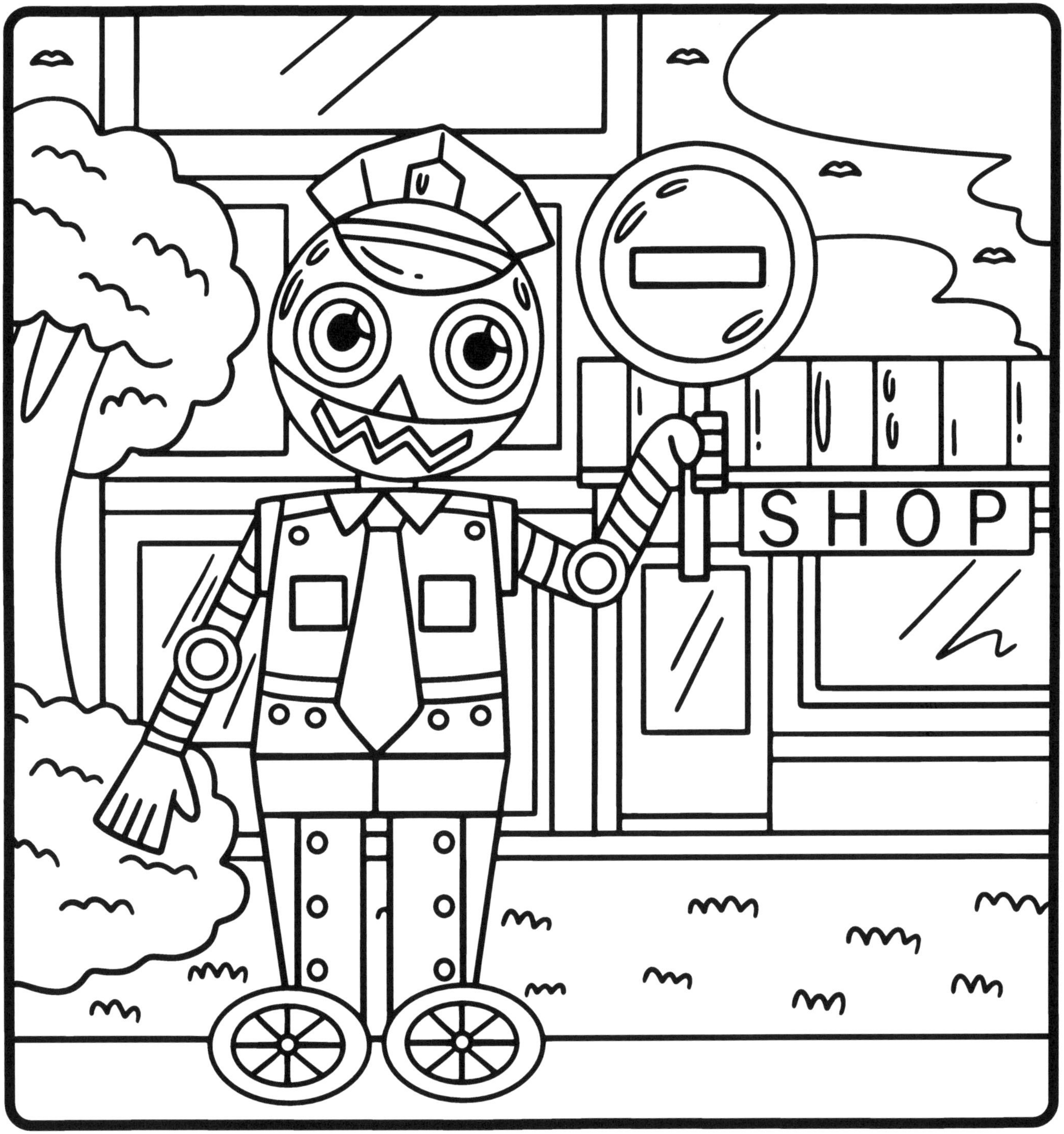
SHOP

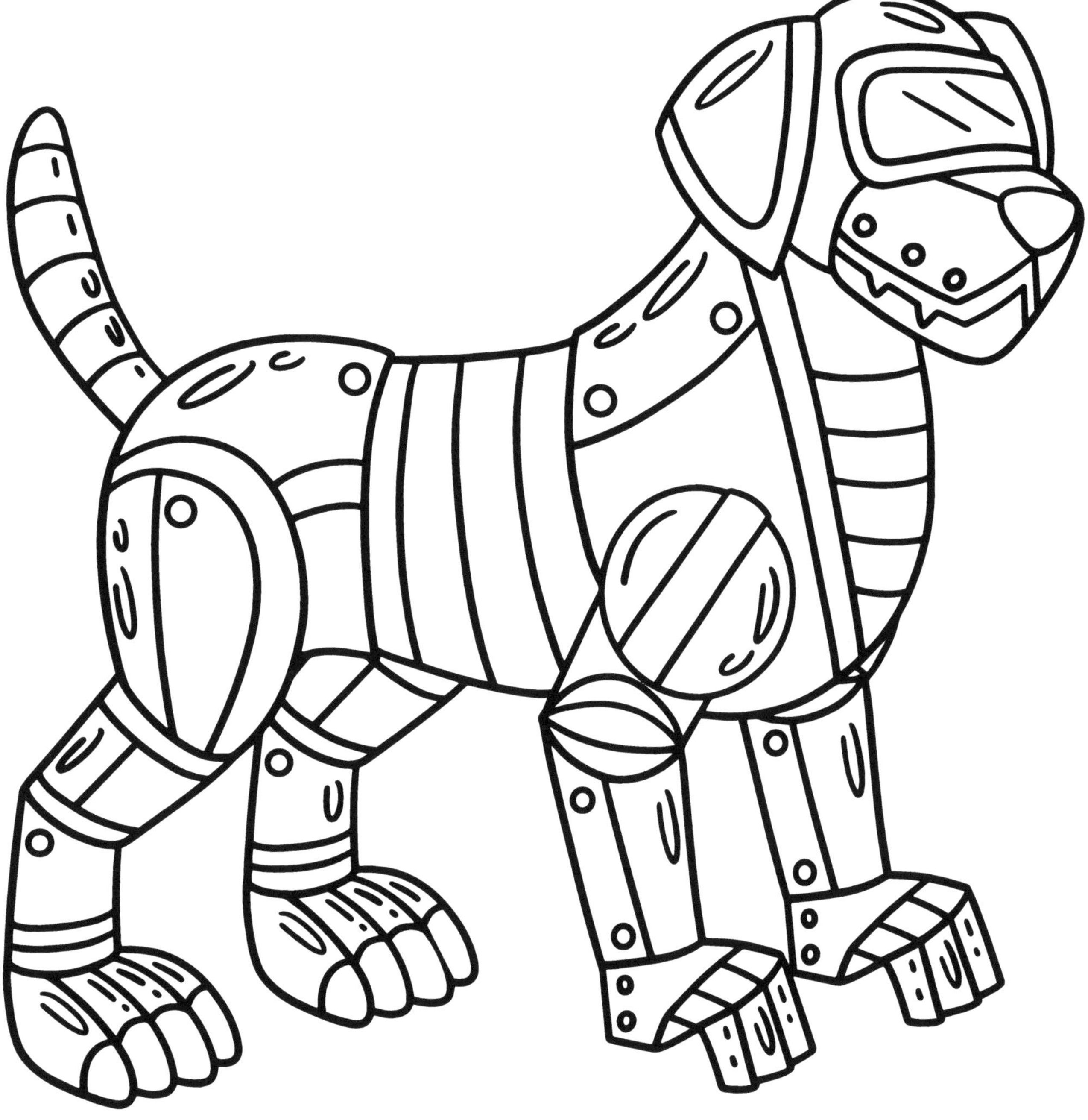

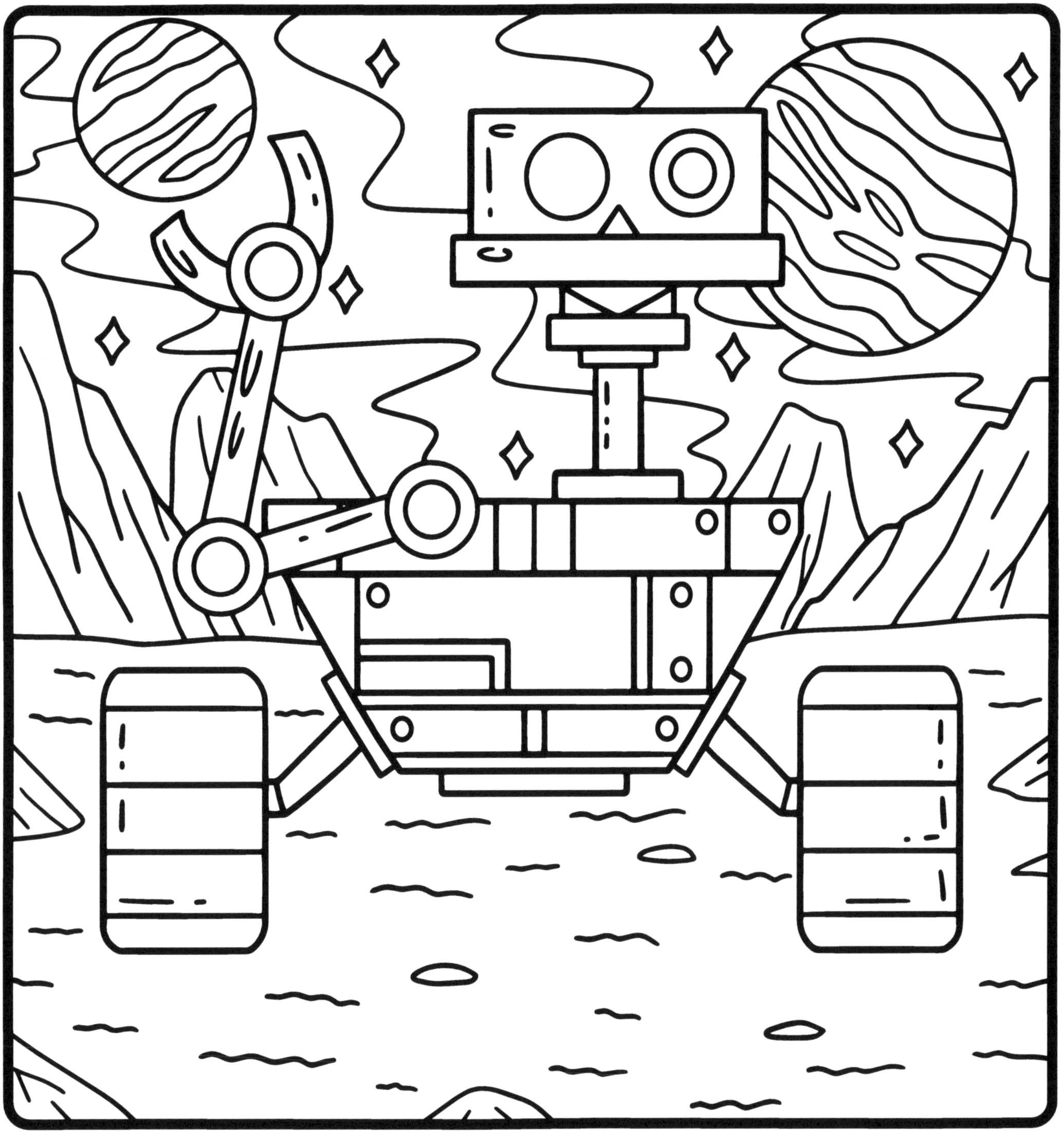

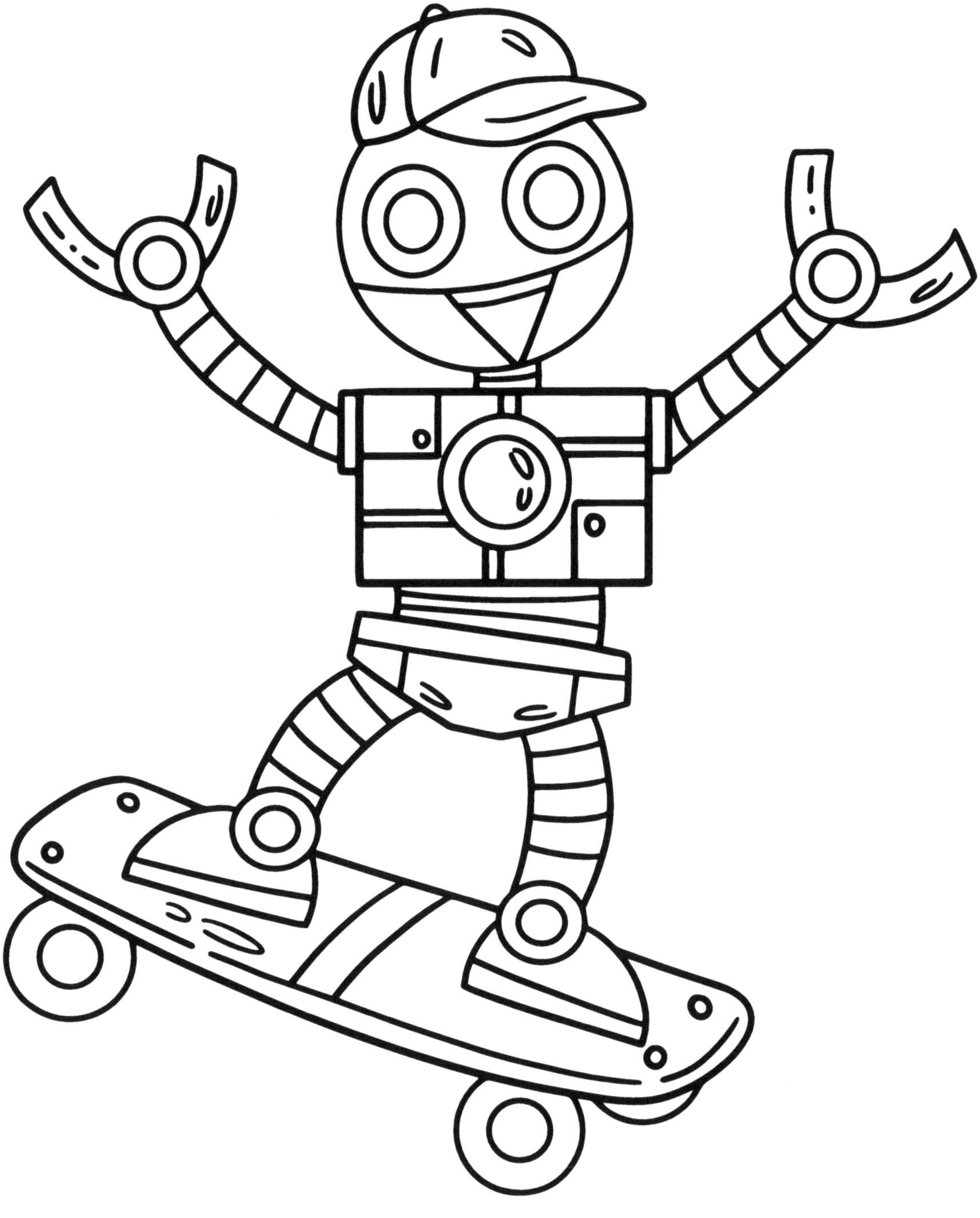

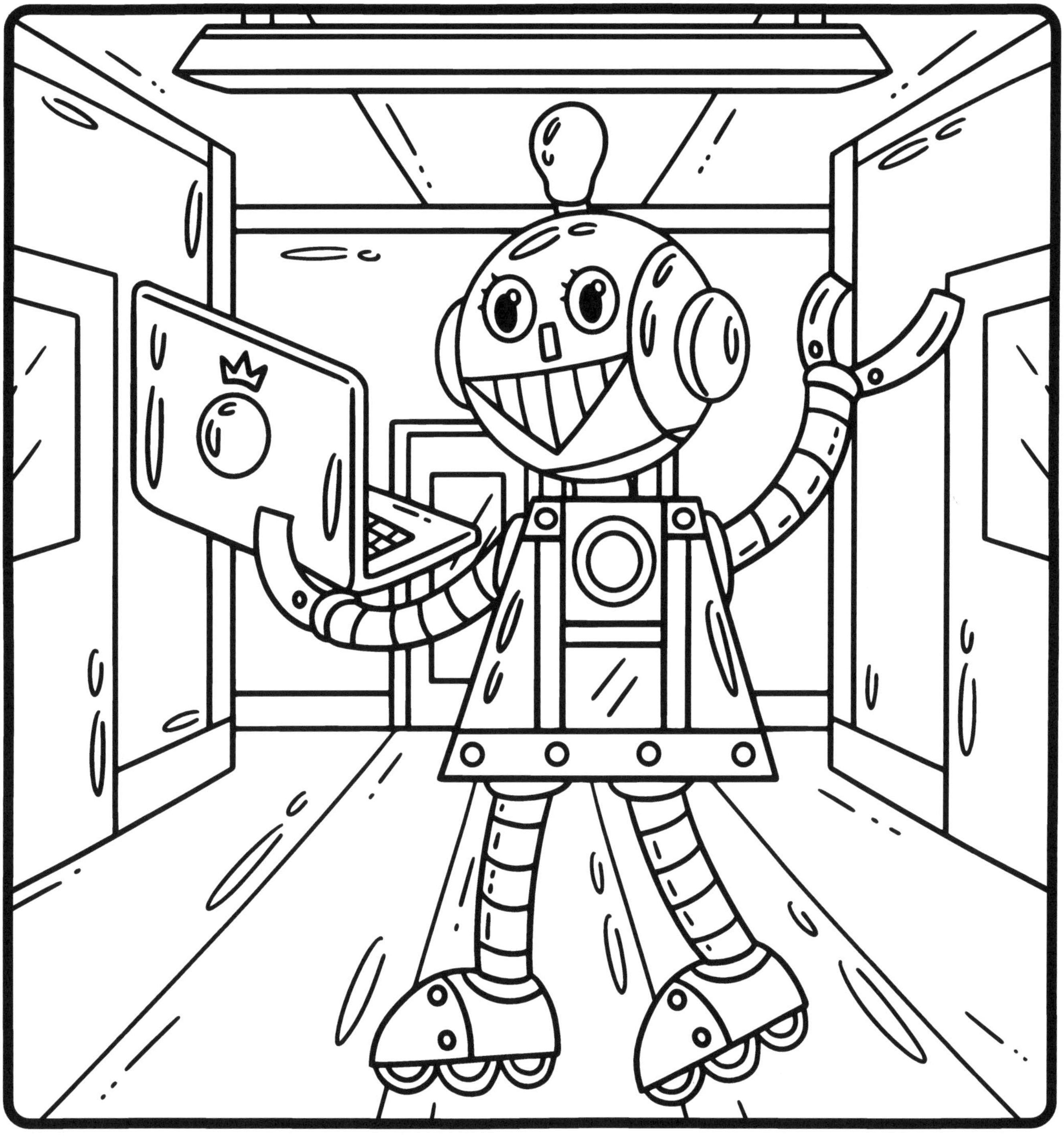

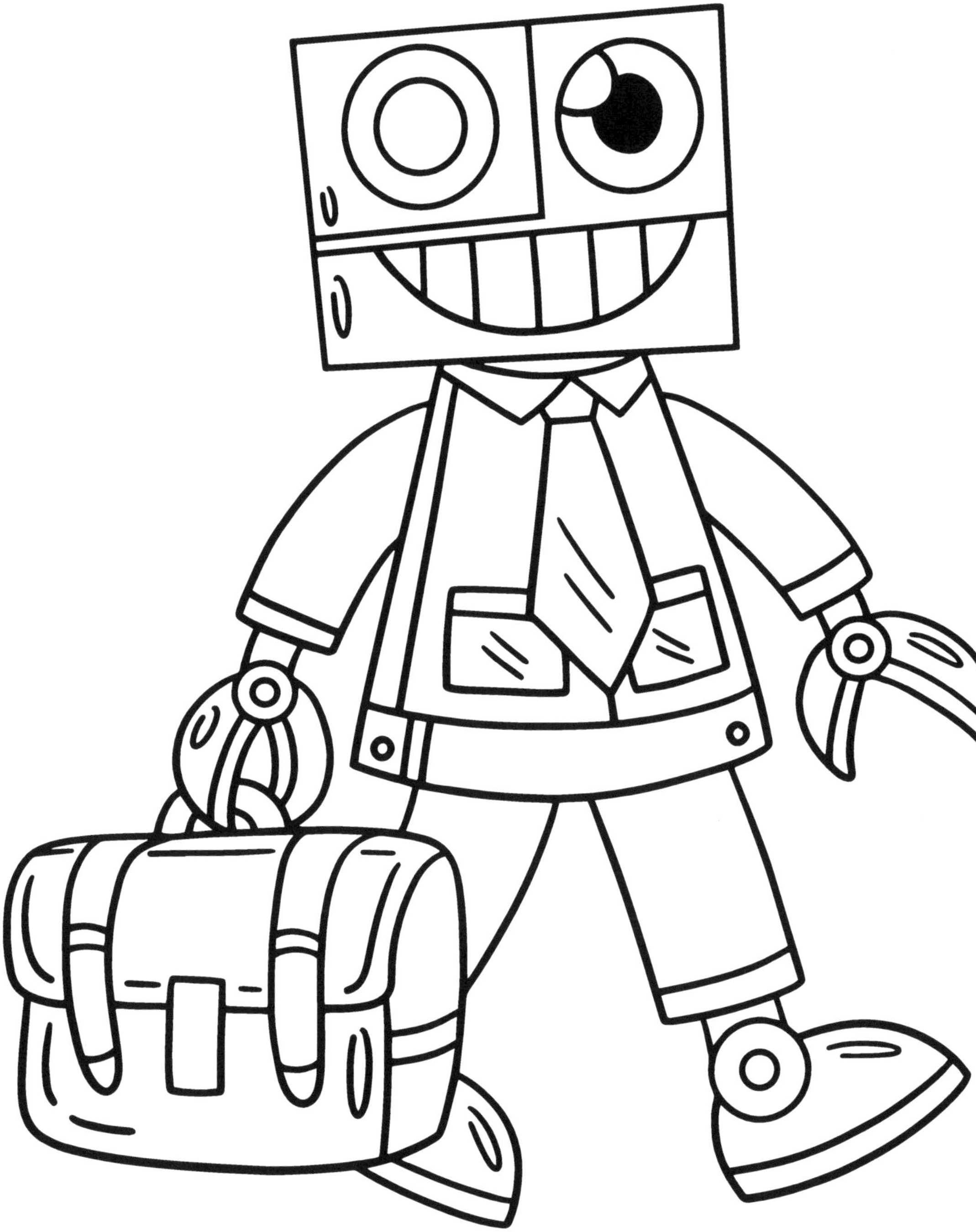

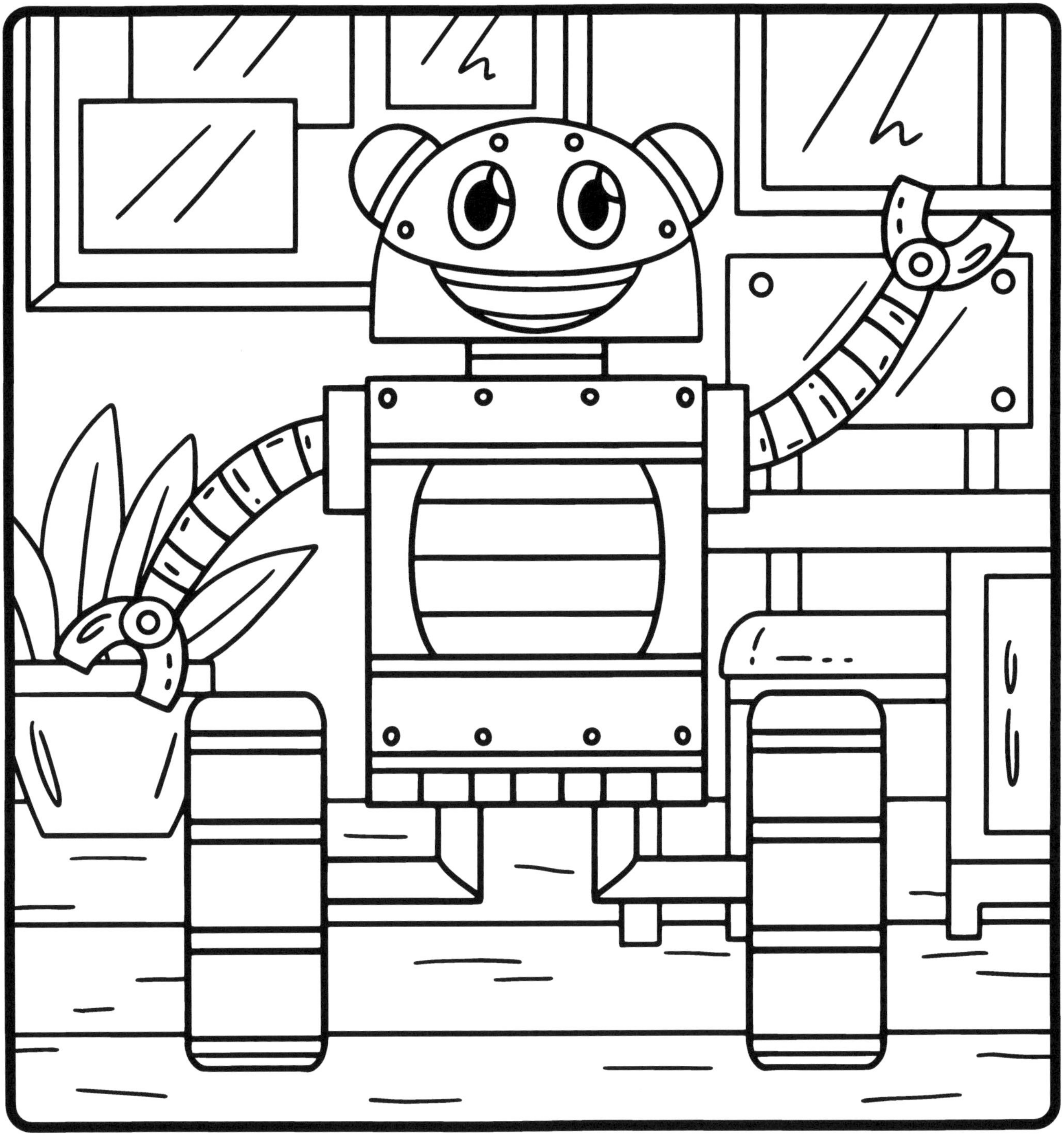

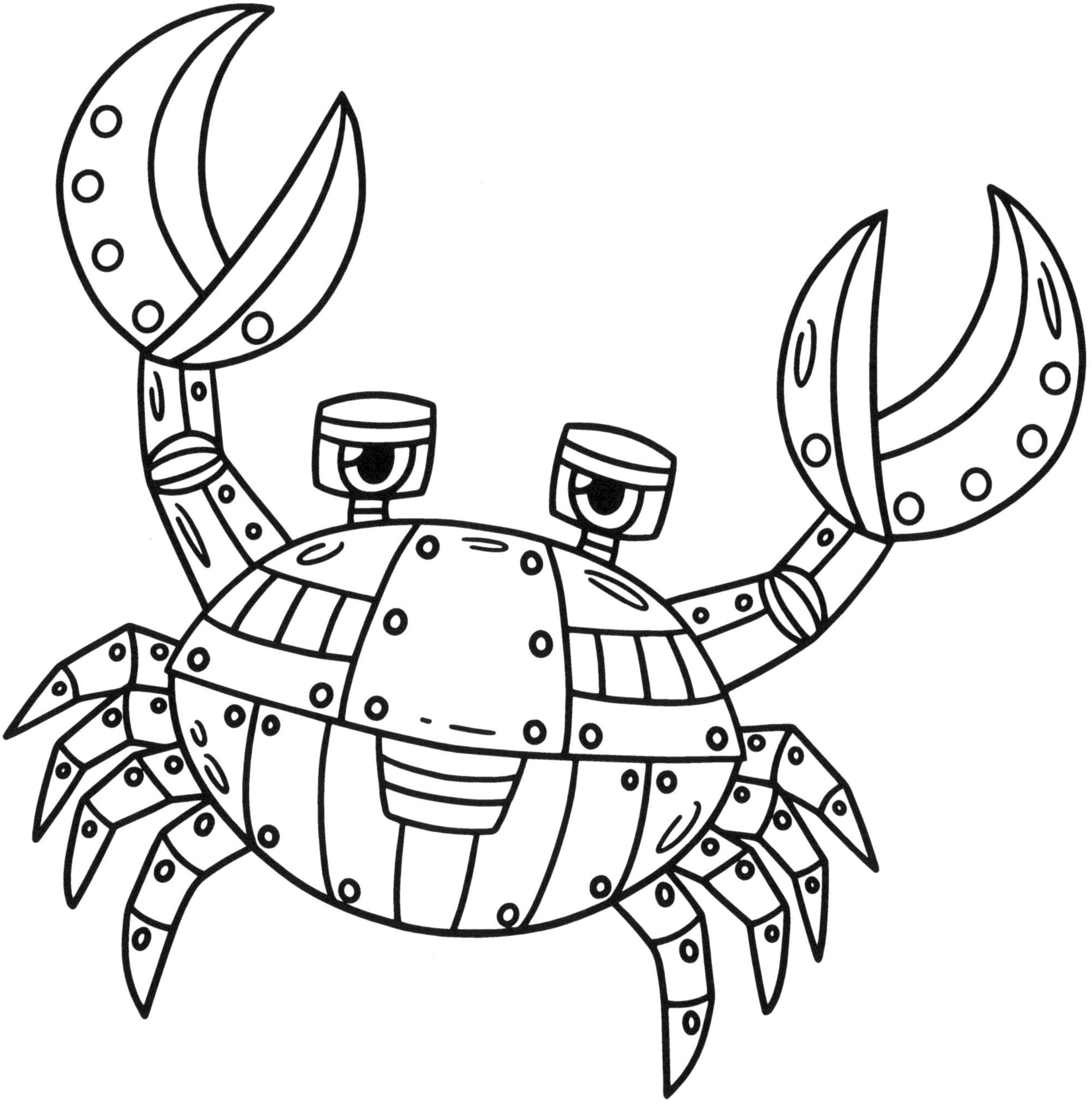

Made in United States
Orlando, FL
02 December 2024

54803095R10057